D1072005

ROMANS
A REVOLUTIONARY
MANIFESTO

Christ was an Aryan. But Paul used his teaching to mobilize the underworld and to organize an earlier Bolshevism.

Adolf Hitler

Wheresoever I open St. Paul's epistles, I meet not words but thunder, and universal thunder, thunder that passes through all the world.

John Donne

ROMANS
A REVOLUTIONARY
MANIFESTO

Lycurgus M. Starkey, Jr.

ABINGDON PRESS
Nashville and New York

LIBRARY — LUTHERAN SCHOOL
OF THEOLOGY AT CHICAGO

BS
2665.2
.S8

ROMANS: A REVOLUTIONARY MANIFESTO

Copyright © 1973 by Abingdon Press

All rights in this book are reserved.
No part of the book may be reproduced in any manner whatsoever
without written permission of the publishers except brief quotations embodied in critical articles or reviews. For information
address

Abingdon Press, Nashville, Tennessee.

Library of Congress Cataloging in Publication Data

STARKEY, LYCURGUS MONROE. Romans: a revolutionary manifesto.
1. Bible. N. T. Romans—Criticism, interpretation, etc. I. Title.
BS2665.2.S8   227'.1'066   73-5870

ISBN 0-687-36604-6

Scripture quotations noted RSV are from the Revised Standard
Version of the Bible, copyrighted 1946, 1952, 1971 by the Division
of Christian Education, National Council of Churches, and are
used by permission.

Scripture quotations noted NEB are from The New English Bible.
© the Delegates of the Oxford University Press and the Syndics
of the Cambridge University Press, 1961, 1970. Reprinted by
permission.

Scripture quotations noted TEV are from the Today's English
Version of the New Testament. Copyright © American Bible
Society 1966.

MANUFACTURED BY THE PARTHENON PRESS AT
NASHVILLE, TENNESSEE, UNITED STATES OF AMERICA

To LaVena Jones Starkey

Prelude

A new title has appeared on the bookstands: *The Sayings of Chairman Jesus*. Why not subtitle the Epistle to the Romans "The Revolutionary Manifesto of Chairman Paul"? For St. Paul's Romans account of the gospel of Jesus Christ, taken seriously (not just superficially), is a foundation shaker. Key figures in Christian history and Western society have been turned on and turned around by it.

Unfortunately, the mind-bending, world-changing character of Jesus' "Godspell" has never been taken seriously by the conventional Christian. And the local church often wraps the power of the gospel in a brown-paper bag. But the Word of the Lord is breaking out of the bag. Many conventional Christians confronted by the Word are dropping out of the church, preferring conventionality to true Christianity. But many others, searching for a new humanity, are seeing anew the revolutionary character of the gospel. The search is going on in local churches, in the youth culture, in councils of churches, in the underdeveloped spiritual world of conventional Christianity.

This book does not advocate violence. *Revolution* has various meanings, as will be seen in chapter 1, and in its nonviolent connotation the term may be accurately applied to St. Paul. The major themes of Paul's manifesto are examined in part 1. Then, in part 2, we look at the lives of some great men who were turned right side up by the Word through Romans. And like the old Salvation Army soldier kneeling at the place of his conversion, we pray, "Do it again, Lord; do it again."

Acknowledgments

My thanks to United Methodist Women who have accepted my teaching ministry throughout the years. A former president of our local church United Methodist Women, Eloise Lewright, typed this manuscript, for which I am most grateful.

Contents

1 Revolution, Religion, and Romans

Revolution: A Fact of Our Time

"Whenever any Form of Government becomes destructive of [the rights of the people], it is the Right of the People to alter or to abolish it, and to institute new Government. . . . When a long train of abuses and usurpations, pursuing invariably the same Object evinces a design to reduce [the people] under absolute Despotism, it is their right, it is their duty, to throw off such Government, and to provide new Guards for their future security." This is not part of a Communist manifesto. Nor is it some revolutionary statement of the World Council of Churches. These words insisting upon the right—indeed, the duty—to rise up against tyranny are from the Declaration of Independence.

Revolution is *our* word. It is part of American history. It is the third and fourth stanzas of "The Star-Spangled Banner"—words our civic clubs might choke on if they sang them as lustily as they sing the only stanza they know. It is Henry Clay, speaking in the House of Representatives on March 24, 1818: "An oppressed people are authorized, whenever they can, to rise and break their fetters." It is Daniel Webster saying, "Repression is the seed of revolution." It is Abraham Lincoln, in his first inaugural address, on March 4, 1861: "If by the mere force of numbers a majority should deprive a minority of any clearly written constitutional right, it might, in a moral point of view, justify revolution—it certainly would if such a right were a vital one."

Not every revolution is successful; not every revolution serves a just cause. A revolution may be no more than a successful effort to get rid of a bad government and set up a worse, as Bernard Shaw observed.

An agitator was addressing the crowd at Speakers' Corner in Hyde Park, where free speech reigns supreme. "Comes the era of the common man," he said, "and you will enjoy the pleasures of the rich. You will walk down Park Lane wearing a top hat—"

"Excuse me," interrupted a member of his working-class audience, "but hi'd rather 'ave a cloth cap."

"—or if you prefer it a cloth cap," went on the speaker. "You'll wear a cutaway coat and pinstripe trousers then."

"Excuse me," interposed the fellow again, "but hi'm more comfertabul in corduroys."

"Very well, corduroys, if you insist," continued the annoyed orator. "And you'll ride to work in a Rolls Royce—"

"Excuse me," said the Cockney, "but hi'd rather use me bike."

The orator left his platform, grabbed the man by the sleeve, and shook him roughly. "Listen, you!" he said between his teeth, "comes the revolution, and you'll do what you are bloody well told to do!" And certainly, the so-called Communist and Fascist revolutions of our century have done just that—failed to grant political freedom and consequently failed in the area of economics as well.

The amazing new factor for us is the way in which the word *revolution* has become again a topic for popular discussion in America, and a serious pursuit for some. In the sixties especially, the meaning of revolution came home to us as never before since the close of the eighteenth century. Oh, we were told in history class and American literature courses about the men at Concord and the "shot heard round the world." We were reminded that many peoples kindled their aspirations at the fires of the American Revolution—especially the demonstration on these shores that the poor need not remain poor. But the more affluent we have become, the less revolutionary, the more reactionary, we are. At least, that is what anti-American Europe sees in us today, and sometimes we almost convince ourselves that it is so.

Although revolution, with its concomitance of violence, is a fearsome word for us, it is a reality in our world today: Cuba, Algeria, Hungary, Latin America, Africa—and now the long-delayed recognition by the West of Red China. Herbert Marcuse's updated Marxism is read on college campuses, and Frantz Fanon's guide to black revolution in Africa has become "must" reading for embittered blacks in the ghettos of the United States. Sixteen Roman Catholic bishops of the Third World—principally the underdeveloped countries of the southern hemisphere—have cried out for distributive justice, and for revolution, if necessary, to get that justice for their peoples. The swing of Roman Catholic leadership in South America from the bastions of privilege to the barrios of poverty is phenomenal. The Colombian guerrilla-priest Camilo Torres, ambushed and killed as he tried to man the machine gun of his ill-fated band, has become a new national hero and a revolutionary martyr for Latin America. With the news of Camilo's death, rioting broke out in Bogotá. Students recklessly roamed through the streets, demanding to see his body. Over television a priest blamed his church for having driven Camilo into the revolutionary camp. And in wretched villages throughout Colombia people shouted, "Camilo lives! Camilo lives!" [1]

So it is not strange that churchmen from the underdeveloped countries, convinced that God is at work in the rise and fall of men and nations, and despairing of needed social reform from tyrannical governments, have turned to theologizing about and participating in revolution. Theology is always situational to some extent, as is the rewriting of history or philosophy. Men must continually appropriate the treasures of the gospel for the needs of the present and future. In 1966 a Conference on Church and Society sponsored by the World Council of Churches at Geneva, Switzerland, brought together representatives from all the major churches around the world. Predominantly laymen from the underdeveloped countries, these Christians tried to hammer out an ecumenical theology of revolution—with mixed results.

Now revolution has come home again to where it all started, to the "land of the free and the home of the

[1] George Celestin, "A Christian Looks at Revolution," in *New Theology No. 6*, ed. Martin E. Marty and Dean G. Peerman (New York: The Macmillan Co., 1969), p. 94.

brave" as our national anthem reminds us. During the sixties American student revolt inspired by Berkeley was exported to France and Germany. We have wrestled with various revolutionary cadres committed to the overthrow of the American system—the Black Panthers, the SDS, the Weathermen. The slogan "Power to the people" and the clenched-fist gesture are recognized as American phenomena. Most of us, including the scholars, do not take these violent threats seriously. But if revolution with violence seems very unlikely in America, certainly the necessity of rapid social change and reform is a clear mark of our time. "The times they are a-changin'" sings Bob Dylan, and Alvin Toffler's best seller warns the uptight ones of us of the "future shock" we must face.

Revolution, American Style

The number one nonfiction best seller in America for many months of 1970 was Yale professor Charles Reich's *The Greening of America*. He asserts:

There is a revolution coming. It will not be like revolutions of the past. It will originate with the individual and with culture, and it will change the political structure only as its final act. It will not require violence to succeed, and it cannot be successfully resisted by violence. It is now spreading with amazing rapidity, and already our laws, institutions and social structure are changing in consequence. It promises a higher reason, a more human community, and a new and liberated individual. Its ultimate creation will be a new and enduring wholeness and beauty—a renewed relationship of man to himself, to other men, to society, to nature, and to the land.[2]

Reich sees the new generation gradually dropping out of all that has gone wrong with the American corporate state alliance between big business and big government, because of a new consciousness, a "new head," a new world view, a new man. While Reich is very critical of America's present subordination of the human to the technological, of the individual to the state, of nature to industry, of participatory democracy to authoritarian hierarchies of decision making, the book is, finally, a testament of hope for our system, which can and will change for what he considers to be the better, without recourse to violence. "Competition, rivalry or personal flights of ego and power have become socially destructive," says Reich. Haven't they always been? we ask. Reich continues: "Given an abundance of material goods, the possibilities of a human community are finally made real, for it is now possible to believe in the goodness of man."

Reich's "Greening of America," as the title suggests, will be a fulfillment of our nation's hopes and dreams, not a self-amputation. The revolution will preserve the best of the past, not destroy it:

From the pre-industrial age it can take the integration and balance of life, the sense of God in everything. From the industrial era it can take technology and the steady rise to a higher level of life. From its own age it can take the control and use of technology, and the way of life of

[2] Charles A. Reich, *The Greening of America* (New York: Random House, 1970), p. 2.

satisfaction, community, and love, a way of life that aspires higher and higher, without forgetting its human source. . . . The new age . . . will not only release but augment and inspire, and make that the chief end of society. And it will do so within a society that makes the Judeo-Christian ethic not merely an ignored command, but a realistic way of life.[3]

Who can argue with this, except to ask for realism? Here is the greatest weakness of Reich's utopian vision —his lack of Christian realism about the inordinate self-centeredness of man.

The movie *Sometimes a Great Notion* is about the Stampers of Oregon, a lumberjack family with a nineteenth-century (Reich's "Consciousness I") mentality. "Never give an inch" was their motto, and they applied it with admirable determination. They would keep their contract with the lumber mills even though their neighbors in the union were starving while striking for higher prices. "To hell with everybody else, and on with our commitments." This didn't keep the Stampers from little acts of mercy toward neighbors in need. But their self-interest was no wider than their own pride and material well-being. The film's theme song is entitled "The Family of Man," and in its call for a wider brotherhood under one Father there is judgment of the Stampers and their rugged individualism. A revolution with a human face needs something more compassionate than "Up the Establishment": a commitment to justice and the political achievement thereof requires the motivation of genuine love for others, for self, for nature, for God.

[3] *Ibid.*, p. 424.

A second recent book on revolution in America comes from abroad. As successful in America as it was in France is Jean-François Revel's *Without Marx or Jesus,* subtitled "The New American Revolution Has Begun." Revel's revelations on American society are intended chiefly for European, and especially French, readers. He punches holes in the smug European anti-Americanism through comparison after comparison with, for example, the pollution, the racism, the muzzled media, and the crisis in the classrooms, which are found in Europe, so that American society comes off smelling like the proverbial rose. The Marxist-Leninist states represent a failure of revolution, says Revel. Their hoped-for economic socialism has miserably bogged down in the repression of political freedom.

A story out of East Germany illustrates this point. Wilhelm Pieck, a Communist leader there, one day met an old woman and asked how she found things. "Terrible," she said. "There is very little to eat and it won't be long before there is nothing to wear." "Cheer up, grandma," said Pieck. "Think of the South Seas. Out there they eat very little and go around naked." "Oh, when did the Russians liberate them?" was her reply.

Revolution in Europe is impossible, according to Revel. Lacking the freedom and openness of the United States, European society is drowning in a sea of compromises. That the Third World is an inevitable ground of revolution is a nostalgic myth, says Revel. Only an economic breakthrough made possible with the help of a truly revolutionary industrial nation can bring about total change in the underdeveloped countries. Japan was canny enough to capitalize on this. The first world revolution to bring freedom and power to the people occurred in England, America, and France in the eighteenth century. It was "the only revolution ever to keep more promises than it broke, and to create a world that more or less conformed, or at least was comparable, to its original ideals. In other words, it was the only revolution, up to the present, to succeed." [4]

Revel's program of revolution is a catalog of mankind's present-day ills:

> the abolition of war and of imperialist relations by abolishing both states and the notion of national sovereignty; the elimination of the possibility of internal dictatorship (a concomitant condition of the abolition of war) ; world-wide economic and educational equality; birth control on a planetary scale; complete ideological, cultural, and moral freedom, in order to assure both individual happiness through independence and a plurality of choice, and in order to make use of the totality of human creative resources.
>
> Obviously this is a utopic program, and it has nothing in its favor, except that it is absolutely necessary if mankind is to survive. [5]

And where will this revolution take place? Listen to the first sentence of Revel's book: "The revolution of the twentieth century will take place in the United States." The French reader picks himself up off the mat, then the second sentence hits him: "It can take place nowhere else." [6] Only in the United States are there

[4] Jean-François Revel, *Without Marx or Jesus*, tr. by Jack Bernard (Garden City, N.Y.: Doubleday & Co., 1971) , p. 79.

[5] *Ibid.*, p. 182.

[6] See Mary McCarthy's Afterword, *ibid.*, p. 243.

five revolutions taking place simultaneously so as to make for one total revolution exportable to the entire world. In this country our French journalist sees political, social, technological, international, and interracial revolutions, and all without violence. It is neither necessary nor desirable to burn down the house to get rid of the ants.

What's in a Name?

At this point perhaps we had better take time out for definition. "Revolution is one of the looser words," said Crane Brinton in the opening line of *The Anatomy of Revolution.*[7] We've used it to mean everything from a palace *coup d'état* to the obvious need for social change. The latter may have been what Thomas Jefferson was referring to in a letter to Samuel Kercheval in 1816, when he wrote that a "revision" in our national life every nineteen years would be desirable. Originally *revolution* meant exactly the opposite of the usual present-day definition. An astronomical term, which gained wider usage in the natural sciences from Copernicus' use of it in *De revolutionibus orbium coelestium,* the word suggested no violent or radical change. The orderly, revolving motion of the stars suggested an eternal, preordained recurrence of patterns in the tides of mortal men. Thus, in its early usage the word, when applied to historical change, really meant *restoration,* like the

[7] Crane Brinton, *The Anatomy of Revolution* (New York: Random House, 1965), p. 3.

restoration of the monarchy after Cromwell in seventeenth-century England. Again, the restoration of Protestant rule in England in 1688 was called the Glorious Revolution—a return to something from the past; the good old days are back again. It was with the American and French revolutions in the latter part of the eighteenth century that the word took on its implication of drastic change. Not a return to the past, but a whole new ball game—this is what the word came to mean. A change not just in political parties, "but a whole new way of living, coming at you, going strong." [8]

"What is revolution?" asks Jürgen Moltmann, professor of theology at Tübingen University in Germany. "I understand revolution to mean a transformation in the foundations of a system—whether of economics, of politics, of morality, or of religion. All other changes amount to evolution or reform." [9] We have already seen that Reich thinks of revolution as involving a change of consciousness, a new perception of reality that involves the total life of man.

A Theology of Revolution

Now if our time is the era of revolutionary change, the transformation of American society, the exportation

[8] See Hannah Arendt, *On Revolution* (New York: Viking Press, 1963) , pp. 35 ff.

[9] Jürgen Moltmann, *Religion, Revolution, and the Future* (New York: Charles Scribner's Sons, 1969) , p. 131.

of a world revolution from these shores to all others, defying once again all the laws of acoustics with a "shot heard round the world," then we desperately need a theology of revolution, an understanding of God's work and our response, in the transformations of our time. Harvey Cox of Harvard said it first, in *The Secular City:* "We are trying to live in a period of revolution without a theology of revolution. The development of such a theology should be the first item on the theological agenda today." [10]

Technology and science have put man on the moon. Technology and science can put bread on the table and provide medical care and education for all, in every village and ghetto. A limiting of the birth rate and a concern about our environment demand a higher place on the nation's priority list. What is needed is the assumption of responsibility, a commitment to try. Man's pride is not his only deadly sin; we need to get up off the backside of our apathy as well. God not only tries to keep us from playing god; he would like to see us play man, to act out our full humanity. Therefore, responsible decision making which can make a difference for mankind has become the focus of theology today. And so, younger theologians such as Harvey Cox, Jürgen Moltmann, and Johannes Metz have sought to show the liberating power of the gospel that can fulfill man's potential as manager of God's creation. A new man, a new life, a new society are all promised in Jesus, who is not only the Alpha but, even more significantly, the

[10] Harvey Cox, *The Secular City* (New York: The Macmillan Co., 1965), p. 93.

Omega, of human existence. As Walter Rauschenbusch, a Baptist slum pastor and professor, said at the turn of the century: "Ascetic Christianity called the world evil and left it. Humanity is waiting for a revolutionary Christianity which will call the world evil and change it." [11] Closer to our own time, the Roman Catholic priest-scientist Teilhard de Chardin says essentially the same: "The world will not be converted to the heavenly promise of Christianity unless Christianity has previously been converted to the promise of the earth."

Romans and the Revolution

Let me suggest that the coming revolution in America and the world needs that divine dynamic found in St. Paul's Epistle to the Romans, one of the most revolutionary manifestos ever written. Put down on papyrus by a little Jewish tentmaker in the back streets of Corinth over nineteen hundred years ago, it has sparked Christian renewal and reformation again and again.

As the last will and testament of St. Paul before his eventual execution by the state for political subversion, the letter contains the essence of the martyr's gospel. Here the great apostle to the Western world explains his Christianity as being independent of the Jewish law. It has the liberating freedom of a new faith as old as Abraham, which delivers men from the sacred laws and cults of religion. These were fighting words, when

[11] Walter Rauschenbusch, *Christianity and the Social Crisis,* ed. R. D. Cross (New York: Harper & Row, Torchbooks, 1964), p. 91.

one considers Paul's struggle in the Jewish synagogues
of the Hellenic Diaspora, and his showdown with the
Jewish Christians in the mother church in Jerusalem.
But Paul and his Romans gospel won the battle, and
Christianity moved out from Judaism to become a world
faith on its own.

Again, the gospel according to Romans changed the
life of a brilliant young profligate of North Africa by
the name of Augustine. After his conversion, and with
the Roman Empire caving in around him, this pastor-
bishop of Hippo wrote a philosophy of history on biblical themes which has served Western man for fifteen
hundred years. Augustine's *City of God* gives a goal and
a model for the ever-changing cities of men.

The revolutionary Word of God spoke to a young
Augustinian monk by the name of Martin Luther
through the Epistle to the Romans: "The just shall live
by faith," faith alone. That liberating word assisted in
the breakdown of feudal autocracies in church and
state, and authored a heritage of hell-raisers searching
for a better country, a holy commonwealth. The Diggers
and Levellers, the Quakers and Puritans, the Separatists
and Baptists were all weaned on Luther's hardscrabble
grit from Romans.

In the eighteenth century Luther's Preface to the
Epistle to the Romans shook up a young Anglican priest
so high-church he nearly strangled in his clerical collar,
and so impractical he made a zealous mess of his chap-
laincy in the Georgia colony. But again, the liberating
word of Romans turned John Wesley around and un-
leashed forces of personal and social change in the
English-speaking world of the eighteenth and nineteenth

centuries. Wesley was liberated from the stifling structures of an established church, and nineteenth-century America was to become Methodist theologically, replacing the dour Calvinism of Colonial Puritanism.

In our own century Karl Barth's commentary on the Epistle to the Romans in 1919 mixed Sören Kierkegaard and St. Paul in such a way as to liberate men from the humanistic totalitarianism of fascism and a bureaucratic world view. Barth thumbed his nose at Hitler and enabled the Confessing Church of Germany to do the same. And today that motivation for a new consciousness of which Charles Reich and Jean-François Revel dream is all present in Romans. God grants us reconciliation as from above, says St. Paul. God also empowers us to be responsible citizens in the horizontal continuum of history. A new model of humanity is given us in Jesus Christ; a new community is promised in the kingdom of God which stands beyond time, beckoning to all our utopian enterprises; a new birth is given to humanize our animal aggression.

In the sixteenth century Luther spoke of a "revolution" which shakes the world when the word of God is liberated from the traditional authority of the church. If we could liberate God's word in Romans from the traditional authority of church commentary today, what a revolution might shake the world anew, providing a "future-shock-absorber" faith in him who is presently at work to make all things new!

Part I
The Main Themes
of Romans

As often as I hear the Epistles of St. Paul, twice a week, or often three or four times, I rejoice each time over this spiritual trumpet, and I exult and am kindled with holy desires, when I hear the voice which is to me so dear and familiar, and then I imagine that I see him living before me, and that I hear him speak.

St. John Chrysostom

2 The Dynamite for Revolution

Romans 1:1–17

Unashamed

"I am not ashamed of the gospel of Christ: for it is the power of God unto salvation to every one that believeth; to the Jew first, and also to the Greek" (Romans 1:16).[1] With these words St. Paul introduces his Epistle to the Romans, his last will and testament before facing the fury of the Jews in Jerusalem and the calculating tyranny of Rome. The Jews had always wanted signs and miracles for proof of God; the Greeks wanted a very sophisticated, intellectual thesis; the Romans wanted cold, naked steel to keep their imperial crown in place. Paul's proclamation that a descendant of David would be raised from the dead and exalted to the right hand of God as king over all[2] (Romans 1:3–5) —this was an offense to everyone. It was a stumbling block, a scandal to the Jews, foolishness to the Greeks (I Corinthians 1:22–24), and treason to the Romans. It is still

[1] Paul's own soteriological credo pointing to the saving significance of the primitive Christian affirmation of the incarnation.

[2] A post-resurrection, pre-Pauline confession of faith in the primitive Christian community—a christological credo, simply stating the humanity-divinity of Jesus Christ.

an offense, this claim that Jesus is the one way to and from God: no impressive display of art, science, politics, just a peasant babe born in a barn with its steaming dung and dumb beasts; no glitter and grace about a carpenter rabbi on a cross between thieves; no battalions and trumpets from the tomb to challenge the imperial legions of Rome. But here was Paul leaning over the balcony of Western civilization, looking down into that opera-house magnificence, the glory that was Greece, the grandeur that was Rome, the pride that was Israel, leaning way over and waving his fist in the air like the college student in the middle of the distinguished lecture on world peace, crying out, "What about Jesus Christ?" Paul had been sneered at, shouted at, and stoned, but hear what he says: "I am not ashamed." Any one of us could start a revolution with that: "I shall not be ashamed of the gospel of Jesus Christ!"

The Gospel of Christ

Indeed, Paul may have invented the word *gospel* for Christian use. The term is used more than sixty times in his letters, the earliest Christian literature preserved. The later "Gospels" and Acts do not use the term so extensively. Romans itself could qualify as "The Gospel According to St. Paul." It was his good news, to be shouted from the housetops, to be expounded and lived in every synagogue and marketplace.

Someone has said that news is anything that makes a woman say, "Good heavens!" How about "Glory to God in the highest, and on earth peace, good will toward men" (Luke 2:14)? Paul had his "special edition," his "extra, extra!" on the streets of Antioch, Ephesus, and Rome—good news, life-changing headlines of God righting wrong, God making friends, God starting man off anew.

> Good Christian men, rejoice,
> With heart and soul and voice;
> Now ye need not fear the grave;
> Jesus Christ was born to save!

"No need to fear that tumor on my lung; let's operate and accept what comes." "No need to fear what people say; what God says is more important." No need to fear the "international imperialism of money," [3] the racism of people in high places, the police power of the state; no need to fear my own fears, my sense of inferiority, my peacock's pride.

George Leigh Mallory spent his life trying to climb Mount Everest and finally died in the attempt, close to the top. Mallory was once asked, "In climbing a mountain have we vanquished an enemy?" "None; only the enemy within ourselves," he replied. "We have seen the enemy," said Pogo, "and it is us." The enemy within has been vanquished by God in Jesus Christ; the mountain of arbitrary self-will is conquered. Humanity is on top and starting down in Christ, and we can be with that victorious party. This is the good news, the gospel Paul proclaims.

[3] Pope Paul VI, *Populorum Progressio*, 1967.

God's Dynamite

"I am not ashamed of the gospel of Christ: for it is the power of God." Paul's Greek word for power is *dynamis*—"dynamite." In an argument between two rather stupid fellows, one stupid fellow concluded, "If you had dynamite for brains, you couldn't blow off your own cap." The dynamite in the gospel can blow men's minds and hearts. Listen: God loves us, the unlovable. He absorbs our hostility in himself as on the cross. God is here with us now. Christ is risen. Nothing can separate us from his loving Spirit. You are important, and don't let anybody tell you or treat you differently. That's dynamite. That's power to the people. No wonder Christianity has been a detonator of revolution: St. Paul overthrowing Judaism; St. Augustine surviving the Fall of Rome and building a new civilization; Martin Luther overthrowing the tyranny of church and empire; John Wesley humanizing the Industrial Revolution; Karl Barth thumbing his nose at Hitler. No wonder the Christian witness and service in Africa, Latin America, and Asia has been a detonator in the worldwide revolution of rising expectations. God loves you. Christ died for you. You are important. Don't let anybody push you around, cut you off, put you down. God's power to the people!

At one time people thought God's power was in the thunder and lightning, the roar of a volcano, the fearsome destruction of war, the earthquake, wind, and fire. But God's word of power is not there. Elijah discovered that centuries ago while hiding in a cave from his enemies. And men have thought that God's word of power was their great structures, cathedrals and sky-scrapers, the giant corporations of church, state, and industry. But God's word of power is not there. Men have thought, as did Judaism, that God's word of power was in the moral law, in doing good and being honest. But God's word of power is not there. The dynamite of God for exploding, clearing out, and building up human life is Jesus Christ and the preaching of Christ. The dynamite of God is the Holy Spirit of Christ, silently surging through our minds, so that we respond to God's love in faith, in trust, in humble acceptance.

> How silently, how silently
>   The wondrous gift is given!
> So God imparts to human hearts
>   The blessings of his heaven.
> No ear may hear his coming,
>   But in this world of sin,
> Where meek souls will receive him, still
>   The dear Christ enters in.

"I am not ashamed of the gospel of Christ: for it is the power of God unto salvation": the silent, awesome dyna-mite of Christmas, Easter, and Pentecost; the coming revolution of consciousness and compassion in the seventies.

> He breaks the power of canceled sin,
>   He sets the prisoner free;
> His blood can make the foulest clean;
>   His blood availed for me.

Put your guilt behind you. God does in Jesus: "Father, forgive them." Put your apathy aside and take hold of your responsibility for this world. God does in Jesus. "My Father works and I work." Put death down. God does in Jesus. "I am the resurrection and the life." Put your fear of "future shock" out of sight. God does in Jesus: "Behold, I make all things new." "The old order changeth, yielding place to new, And God fulfils himself in many ways." Tennyson wrote these words over a century ago, and they are a gospel for the years ahead. The God who changes us and changes history in Jesus Christ is with us. Hold on to him and be a part of his transformation, his salvation, his change.

Believers All

"I am not ashamed of the gospel . . . : for it is the power of God unto salvation to every one that believeth; to the Jew first, and also to the Greek." Do you realize how revolutionary these last words were in the first century, when everybody thought they were the chosen people? God bless Mom and Pop, me and mine, a few others, and that's all. God bless us Americans and damn you Russians. God bless us white folk and damn all the other colors. God bless us middle-class affluent and damn the poor. That's theological language—but not in the Christian context. St. Paul turned that world upside down—or right side up. He challenged the Jewish establishment within the Christian community in Jerusalem, disobeyed what had been his and their Jewish rites of circumcision, food laws, and temple worship, and took the gospel to the Greeks, to the ends of the earth, to all people. "Salvation for every one that believeth—the Jew *and* the Greek. Why get excited about the Communist *Internationale:*

> Arise, ye prisoners of starvation!
> Arise, ye wretched of the earth.
> For justice thunders condemnation,
> A better world's in birth.

St. Paul said it all in the name of Jesus Christ in the first century. Christians in our own century continue to discover the dynamite of the gospel with St. Paul.

It was dynamite for Dietrich Bonhoeffer, who worked underground with the Confessing Church in Germany and then took part in an abortive plot to kill the Fuehrer. Awaiting trial and death in a Nazi prison, he wrote letters which have suggested new theological directions for Christians. The gospel liberated Dietrich Bonhoeffer from his inward-looking focus on his own soul to an outward-responsible role in society. The power of God in Jesus Christ moved him off the fence and into the fracas.

Jesus Christ is dynamite for Daniel Berrigan. A Roman Catholic priest, Berrigan served time for pouring blood on draft records in Catonsville, Maryland. He registered his Christian conscience against a coercive military conscription which denies young men their freedom of choice and gives them only the freedom to kill. There is another point of view, and many of the young have willingly served in the army. But over three hundred are in prison, one hundred thousand have fled to Canada, over fifty thousand are dead, and two hundred thousand are living with their stumps and eye patches. Daniel Berrigan could not go along or sit on the fence. The power of the gospel led him to get involved. Christ has come, and that can be dynamite if you let it.

A young couple recently gave to their first son at Christian baptism the name Dietrich Daniel. The new day is coming. The new day is here.

One of the many humorous stories surrounding Abraham Lincoln concerns his suggested appointment of the Rev. Dr. Shrigley of Philadelphia as a chaplain for Congress. A delegation called on President Lincoln to protest that the man was not "sound in his theological opinions. He does not believe in endless punishment but believes that even the rebels will be saved."

"Well, gentlemen, if that be so," replied Lincoln, "and there is any way under heaven whereby the rebels can be saved, then, for God's sake and their sakes, let the man be appointed."

The debate over universalism began with St. Paul's letter to the Romans, chapters 9–11. But there is no debate in Paul or in subsequent Christian history concerning the centrality of Christ.

The man appointed for our salvation is Jesus Christ. That's dynamite!

3 One Hell of a World

Romans 1:18—3:20

"I have already charged that all men, both Jews and Greeks, are under the power of sin" (Romans 3:9 RSV).

Peter Cook and Dudley Moore give us a sophomore's version of St. Paul the killjoy, a version most sophomores learn from their biblically illiterate professors:

Dud: I think St Paul's got a bloody lot to answer for.
Pete: He started it, didn't he?
Dud: All those letters he wrote.
Pete: To the Ephiscans.
Dud: You know, "Ah, dear Ephiscans, ah, stop enjoying yourself, God's about the place."
Pete: "Signed Paul." You can imagine it, can't you? There's a nice Ephiscan family, settling down to a good breakfast of fried mussels and hot coffee, and they're just sitting there, and it's a lovely day outside, they're thinking of taking the children out, ye know, for a picnic, by the sea, by the lake and have a picnic there, and everything's happy, the sun coming through the trees, birds are chirping away.
Dud: Boats bobbing on the ocean.
Pete: The distant cry of happy children.
Dud: Clouds scudding across the sky.

Pete: Naturally, Dud—in fact an idyllic scene is what you call it, when suddenly into the midst of it all—tap, tap, tap, on the bloody door.

Dud: What's that?

Pete: You know what it is?

Dud: No.

Pete: It's a messenger bearing a letter from Paul. They rush to the door to open it, thinking it may be good news— perhaps grandfather's died and left them a vineyard. They open it up and what do they discover? "Dear George and Deirdre and family, stop having a good time, resign yourself not to have a picnic, cover yourself with ashes and start flailing yourselves."

Dud: "Till further notice."

Pete: "Signed Paul." [1]

Alienation Everywhere

Is St. Paul too negative about human nature in the first three chapters of Romans? I know we are not so naïve as to believe, as we once did, that man is on an up-escalator of moral progress—"every day, in every way, we are getting better and better." But to say that all mankind is sinful and deserving of hell, the people of God as well as the people of the world; to say that mankind has exchanged the truth about God for a lie, worshiping the created rather than the Creator, and that hence we live a lie, a perversion in all our other

[1] From Peter Cook and Dudley Moore, *Dud and Pete* (London: Methuen & Co., 1971). Used by permission of the publishers.

relationships—that's a little strong. Mankind is one big credibility gap—that's what St. Paul says.

Art Linkletter tells of a sign on the front of a little Baptist church near his house in Beverly Hills, that reads, "If you're tired of sin—come in." Underneath was written, in a female hand, "If you ain't, call Freda, 253-0001." There's the gap between what we might be and what we are.

The December, 1971, issue of *Rotarian* magazine was devoted entirely to what children think about the world. Many of their sobering estimates sound like the first three chapters of Romans. Marie Gale, age eleven, of Australia, writes:

> A world of sophistication.
> Tumbling confusingly,
> Hypnotised,
> into developing
> beyond our mental knowledge.
> Separated into nations
> fighting with hatred
> against each other.
> Each independently
> governing themselves
> Not!
> living together as the world
> but as individuals.
> Each better and greater
> than any other nation.
> A notorious world
> of scientific investigations
> leaving the poor
> bewildered and
> smothered in starvation.
> Caring only for themselves

forgetting
the poverty-stricken world
beyond their wealth.[2]

Steve Dobry, age twelve, of the United States, drew a
cartoon of two Martians coming down in their space-
ship to visit the earth, only to see earthmen wearing
gas masks in the street while the Gas Mask Manufactur-
ing Company and the downtown office building of the
Fight Pollution Campaign belch forth smoke into the
atmosphere. Dead fish stink on a derelict swimming
beach, a hypodermic needle of drugs splits the city, hip-
pies rob a jewelry store, tanks fire at each other, and a
peace sign gathers cobwebs. "Here lies the world," says a
tombstone, "—Rest in peace." Underneath the cartoon
are the words presumably said by the Martians: "It's a
nice place to visit, but I wouldn't want to live there."
That's a grim picture from a twelve-year-old, as grim as
Romans 1–3 where St. Paul says this is one hell of a
world and mankind is in desperate shape.

Of course, our tendency is to argue for the good in
man, the righteousness in ourselves, the nobility of human accomplishments—Westminster Abbey, the Nobel
Prize, Americans on the moon, and the conquest of
polio. We take pride in our nation, our party, our race,
our city, our club, our churches and schools. This was
just the kind of defense being offered by the teachers
of religion and ethics in Jesus' own day, and he called
them imposters: "You clean the outside of your cup
and plate, while the inside is full of things you have

[2] "The World" by Marie Gale. *Rotarian*, December, 1971, p. 22.

gotten by violence and selfishness. Blind Pharisee! Clean what is inside the cup first, and then the outside will be clean too!" (Matthew 23:25-26 TEV).

Long before Sigmund Freud and psychoanalysis, Jesus pointed to the inside of the cup, full of violence and hatred toward ourselves, toward others, toward God. Through the centuries the church has encouraged the cure of souls by confession, each individual emptying his own cup so that sins admitted might enable changed behavior and God's pardon. Then in this century Sigmund Freud developed a similar technique for emptying our cup of poison that is repressed and often forgotten. We now have it on medical authority that the corruption within us determines the way we look at ourselves and behave.

A flashily dressed young woman was on the stand in a casualty case. The lawyer for the insurance company, hoping to confuse or irritate her into a contradictory statement, sneeringly asked her, "And when the elevator started to fall, I suppose all the sins of your past flashed before you?" "Don't be absurd," she said. "The elevator only fell nine stories." It would take a lot more time than any psychiatrist or confessor has, for any of us to empty the inside of our cup so that our lives could stand before us and we could deal with and change what is unwelcome there. We see the outside of the cup and largely judge other people that way. Sometimes we can peer over the brim into another person's life, see a little of what is within. And sometimes we can understand ourselves and our own motives better than at other times. But we cannot see into the bottom of our own cup. So people who, like the Pharisees of Jesus' day, go around proclaiming their own merit and righteousness as somehow being above criticism or reproach are, on the evidence of the gospel, *most suspect*. Jesus was sympathetic to the little tax collector in church who beat on his chest and said, "God have pity on me, a sinner." In contrast there was the pious Pharisee who in disdain looked over from a neighboring pew and said loud enough for people all around to hear, "God, I am really a great guy, not like that dirty crum bum." There was no pride in his family—he had it all.

The Wrath Within

Jesus our Lord and St. Paul bring us and all the accomplishments of human civilization, with its mingling of good and evil, under the judgment of another. God looks on the outside of our cup and the inside of our cup clear to the bottom, and sees our world from the viewpoint of eternity. Part of that judgment takes place now. Paul speaks frequently of the wrath of God as if it were an impersonal moral rectifier within the process of history, a kind of inevitable punishment of sin in our moral universe. The sins of the fathers are visited on the children and grandchildren like the radioactive fallout and DDT that poison future generations yet unborn. Back in the 1950s a black woman on a bus was told by the driver, "Get in the back." She was heard to mumble, "God, you must be getting awfully tired of this." He was tired, and we are paying for our sins of the fifties in the seventies. What price are we now paying for permissive, self-indulgent homes with a generation of children who have little reason to honor their mothers and fathers? For sin, we pay and pay and pay, punished by our sins and not just for them. This is the inevitable wrath of God in this hell of a world.

People do continue to hate and cheat neighbors and friends, to fight and feud, steal and murder, quite sure that they can do it in the name of heaven. We frequently try to baptize our inhumanity with some righteous cause as if God were on our side. The popular "One Tin Soldier" makes this point. But after all the citizens of one valley have been killed for their treasure by the citizens of another valley greedy for gain, the treasure vault is found to contain only the words Peace on Earth. The ballad concludes with a note of judgment. There are no angels' trumpets blowing on a final Judgment Day. Only one tin soldier walks away from the bloody battle. Everybody else is dead. What is this but the wrath of God overturning evil, visiting our sins upon us right now?

Court of Final Appeal

In addition to the wrath of God within history, St. Paul insists on a final judgment beyond history. In a "Peanuts" cartoon strip, Linus says to Charlie Brown, "I have a theological question. When you die and go to heaven, are you graded on a percentage or on a curve?"

"On a curve, naturally," says Charlie Brown.

"How can you be so sure?"

"I'm always sure about things that are a matter of opinion." St. Paul insists that each and all will be summoned before a final judgment, when we will be graded by God through Jesus Christ, neither on a percentage nor on a curve. We will not be judged by comparisons with our neighbors or enemies, by our memberships and memorials. God will not look over our medals, degrees, or diplomas as we stand naked before him. The cup of our lives, the vast cup of love and hate which is human history, is measured from a much larger perspective—God's justice and righteousness, and his alone:

> Day of wrath, that day of burning
> Seer and Sibyl speak concerning
> All the world to ashes turning
> Dies irae, dies illa.

Does that sound terribly medieval to you? It sounds pretty modern to me. For unless the final meaning of things rests with God who lays bare the secrets of men's hearts, upon God's judgment and justice, then the whole world is a monstrous sham, an absurd waste of time.

One of El Greco's Crucifixions shows two worshiping patrons kneeling on the ground before the cross. Their unctuous piety is portrayed just as they probably hoped it would look to the world. Is that the final meaning of things—that the wealthy can don the clothes of fashion and pay an artist to immortalize them as pious men before God? But behind the donors there looms a vivid sky, angry, menacing, turbulent—a vast threat to what one critic has called their "showy self-righteousness." Do you sense that threat, that deep questioning of all you claim for yourself? Faith comes precisely at the moment when we are ready to stop arguing about what a clean cup we are, when we are ready to surrender our own claims to righteousness. Saving faith says, "Nothing in my hand I bring; simply to thy cross I cling." "Just as I am, without one plea, but that thy blood was shed for me." Here repentance and faith begin.

What revolutionary drive is there in Sartre's brave willing in the face of the absurd, and his belief that there is no meaning to life unless we put it there? What new consciousness explodes from Harvey Cox's fear that man will be more milquetoast than titan? If man is so much in the driver's seat as to give life its own meaning, if God has been waiting for the hands and feet of his creature to fill up his own inadequacies, we still face the massive resistance and inertia of sin. The Communist understanding of a dialectical materialism operative in history is more purposeful than that. How much greater is the revolutionary thrust of him who looks to the ultimate norms of God's justice and righteousness, the siren call of the coming kingdom already present in Jesus and hence presently involved in transforming history! Even the revolutionary needs to be aware that his new order and ideology are under judgment—the divine criticism as well as a human one.

Reinhold Niebuhr left us this insightful estimate of the Christian community under judgment:

> The Christian church is a community of hopeful be lievers, who are not afraid of life or death, of present or future history, being persuaded that the whole of life and all historical vicissitudes stand under the sovereignty of a holy, yet merciful, God whose will was supremely

revealed in Christ. It is a community which does not fear the final judgement, not because it is composed of sinless saints but because it is a community of forgiven sinners, who know that judgement is merciful if it is not evaded. If the divine judgement is not resisted by pretensions of virtue but is contritely accepted, it reveals in and beyond itself the mercy which restores life on a new and healthier basis.[3]

The possibility of a community of real human transformation, restoring life on a new and healthier basis, "a community that submits its eschatological hopes and utopian models to divine judgment"—here is the potential revolutionary cadre of renewal within this hell of a world.

[3] Reinhold Niebuhr, *Faith and History* (New York: Charles Scribner's Sons, 1949), p. 238.

4 Acceptance from Above

Romans 3:21—8:39

God's Way of Righting Wrong

Some years ago a young Korean student at the University of Pennsylvania stepped out of his apartment to mail a letter at the corner. As he turned from the mailbox, this young leader in student Christian affairs at the university was jumped by a gang of teenage thugs. The eleven black-jacketed boys beat him senseless with lead pipe and brass knuckles. The young Korean never got up again. When the story hit the newspapers all Philadelphia cried out for vengeance. The district attorney secured legislation so that the attackers could be tried as adults. This would have permitted the death penalty, if they were convicted. Then a letter was received from the young man's parents and relatives in Korea. It read in part:

> Our family has met together and we have decided to petition that the most generous treatment possible within the laws of your government be given to those who have committed this criminal action. . . . In order to give evidence of our sincere hope contained in this petition, we have decided to save money to start a fund to be used for the religious, educational, vocational and social guidance of the boys when they are released. . . . We have dared to express our hope with a spirit received from the Gospel of our Saviour Jesus Christ who died for our sins.

This is *God's way of righting wrong*, that amazing paradox of guilt and grace, that great "nevertheless" from above which breaks in upon our hell of a world. In Romans 1:18–3:20 St. Paul has just finished the most scathing denunciation of the sin of man. Not only do we attack and kill and cry vengeance in the streets of Rome and Philadelphia; but all this distortion of humanity proceeds from the way each one of us thumbs his nose at God. But now, nevertheless, in spite of all this, God accepts us, though we are unacceptable. This is the gospel of our Savior Jesus Christ, who died for our sins.

In Romans 3:23–25 (NEB) Paul uses three different metaphors to explain God's way of righting wrong through Christ.

Justification

First, says St. Paul, "all alike have sinned . . . and all are justified by God's free grace alone." *Justification* was a term from the courts and the practice of law. Imagine a courtroom as large as this universe, with the holy God of all creation sitting as judge of all that he has made. This is not just imagining; it is a fact. God is our Judge. The Chinese Communists forgot this fact when they liquidated millions of peasants, took over the land, and forced farmers into agricultural communes. We Americans forgot this fact when we deceived, betrayed, and exterminated the American Indians—men, women, and children—for the sake of their land. We need not indict nations only. Let us take an honest look at ourselves as individuals—our own apathy and greed,

LIBRARY — LUTHERAN SCHOOL
OF THEOLOGY AT CHICAGO

our hostility and pride, and most of all our blasé indifference to the Lord of life. God is our Judge. We are in the prisoner's dock, you and I with all the rest of mankind, the Chinese and the Americans, yellow, black, red, and white—"all alike have sinned"—arraigned before a jury of humanity's conscience. Before God we know we are guilty. Caiaphas and Pilate, Judas and Peter are all there in the prisoner's dock with us—all guilty of continuing to crucify our Creator, and all he intends for his creation.

The tense moment comes for the Divine Judge to pass sentence. Will the defendants stand? We stand with all the rest to hear the penalty. The penalty is death—real death. Politicians may toast each other in the great hall of the people and talk of brave new worlds, but that which defies God and crucifies his Christ has no future, no immortality; it lasts for a day and a night, but it lives only to die.

After passing sentence of death, the Divine Judge does a miraculous thing. He asks the prisoners to step aside, removes his own robes of office, and steps down from his bench. He takes our place to receive the very sentence which he had passed on those convicted of the crime. The Divine Judge offers himself in Jesus to be judged in our place. The sentence is served. Christ is executed. God takes our guilt upon himself. Justice is preserved.

> Was it for sins that I have done,
>   He suffered on the tree?
> Amazing pity! Grace unknown!
>   And love beyond degree.

We are justified, acquitted, by God's free grace alone.

Liberation

Then St. Paul speaks of God's "act of liberation [redemption] in the person of Christ Jesus." A conquering hero-savior wages a war of liberation against man's ancient enemies. The cross is the final battle. Christ wins the victory. The death grip of evil is broken. We prisoners of war can come home. We are liberated.

J. B. Priestley tells of entering the roofless, bombed-out cathedral of Coventry, England, just after World War II. He saw there a large black cross, made out of charred wood. Carved in stone behind the cross were two simple words: "Father, forgive." "That was all," said Priestley, "and it was quite enough. If there is a nobler war memorial than this ruined cathedral, one that drives harder at the shell of chicanery, hypocrisy or self-deceit in which we encase our hearts, I have to see it. Father, forgive! And outside in the streets they were selling the papers that told the same old story of indifference, drift, mischief, prejudice, passion and blind idiocy." Priestley knew that the war against evil still goes on in our world; but somehow what happened on Golgotha means that evil as a force in human life is broken. It may persist, but it persists as a defeated enemy. It will not have the last word in God's world again.

An artist's conception of some huge fourteen-by-thirty-feet faceted glass windows to be erected in a new downtown chapel was exciting. They affirmed the centrality of Christ in the heart of the city. There was the star of David, and God's deliverance of the Jews from bondage

in Egypt—"Let my people go." There were the words of
Martin Luther King's great sermon, "Free at last."
Another note of Christian liberation was marked up in
the title of Pope John XXIII's encyclical *Pacem In
Terris*, "Peace on Earth." Embracing all this was a
regnant figure of the risen Christ, the conquering Lord
of all, with the first and last letters of the Greek alpha-
bet emblazoned on his breast. The nail prints of Calvary
are still in his hands and feet. But now, victorious over
all that tries to put down man, he reaches out those
great arms to enfold all mankind, saying, "I am Alpha
and Omega. . . . I am he that liveth, and was dead; and,
behold, I am alive for evermore, Amen; and have the
keys of hell and of death."

Do you recall Reginald Heber's Lenten hymn?

> The Son of God goes forth to war,
> A kingly crown to gain;
> His bloodred banner streams afar;
> Who follows in his train?

Expiation

Paul's third word for the atonement is *expiation*
(propitiation): "For God designed him to be the means
of expiating sin by his sacrificial death, effective through
faith." Sin is like a pollution of filth which must be
filtered out and cleansed away, an infection which must
be isolated and disinfected, a poison to be counteracted.
Lady Macbeth tries desperately to wash the stain of
Duncan's blood from her hands, just as Pilate had tried

to become clean. We feel we must do something to make things right, to rid ourselves of the infection so that we may enter God's company again. The prophet Micah asks what it takes for guilty man to make things right with God—some sacrifice of animals, a gift of conscience money to atone, some costly offering like one's own child?

On Israel's Day of Atonement, Yom Kippur, certain rituals helped the Jewish people to disinfect their pollution and come to at-onement with God again. The priest sacrificed a pure lamb whose blood was sprinkled on the altar of God. The blood meant life—the life of the lamb, the life of the people offered and reunited with God. Paul was thinking of this when he said that God put forward Jesus as "the means of expiating sin by his sacrificial death." God provided the sacrifice himself, the "one full, perfect, and sufficient sacrifice for the sins of the whole world" as we say in the sacrament of Holy Communion. The blood of Jesus disinfects, and makes up for what we owe.

The movie *Ben Hur* was one of the best motion-picture presentations of the story of Christ I have ever seen. The crucifixion was depicted with special restraint and yet great power. You never saw the face of Christ, but you could hear the soldiers nailing spikes through flesh and bone. You could see the blood trickling down the side of the cross; you could read on the faces of the disciples the bewilderment and disillusionment that he who had been so obedient to God should die like a common criminal. All nature seemed to shout its protest in the crashes of thunder and the flashes of lightning that tore open the sky. A deluge of rain flooded down the hillside, rain mingled with blood. As the angry storm subsides, two leper women who believe in Jesus are cowering in the cave of their imposed quarantine. Suddenly they look at each other's hands and faces, and discover that they have been cleansed of their dread disease. We expect miracles in the aftermath of Calvary—miracles of new life, courage to face the apathy and crassness of those we depend on daily, strength to be new men and women overcoming deep set patterns of pettiness and pride, the willingness to love others as he loved us. All this comes by faith in him: justification and acquittal for the guilty, liberation for the enslaved, expiation for a soiled and separated spirit.

"Thanks be to God through Jesus Christ our Lord!" (Romans 7:25 RSV).

Surely here is the freedom to deal creatively with the many new situations which confront us today. "If God be for us, who can be against us?" We are freed from the notion of restricting the church to four cozy walls to become street Christians. We are freed from the political bag to seek that piety of personal life and habit which taps the wellsprings of divine motivation. God's acceptance in Christ helps us withstand the temptation of peers and profits:

> Let goods and kindred go,
> This mortal life also;
> The body they may kill:
> God's truth abideth still;
> His kingdom is forever.

God's acceptance in Christ faces us forward with responsibility for "thy kingdom come, thy will be done, on earth as it is in heaven."

Emerson once said, "Every revolution was first a thought in one man's mind." Acceptance from above can give us that renewing of the mind, that energizing of the will, so necessary to a personal and social revolution in our time.

5 Can the Jews Be Saved?

Romans 9—11

> Who was the guilty?
> Who brought this upon thee?
> Alas, my treason,
> Jesus, hath undone thee!
> 'Twas I, Lord Jesus,
> I it was denied thee;
> I crucified thee.[1]

The words of this seventeenth-century German hymn for Christians to sing in public worship make it very clear who the Christ-killers are. All mankind is guilty—Jews and Gentiles, you and me. This is basic Christian doctrine.

Looking for a Scapegoat

And yet the curious heresy of a scapegoat to get us off the hook for crucifying God continues to plague Jewish-Christian relations. Judas, perhaps, or Judaism as a whole, has been singled out and persecuted as the God-killer in particular. This scapegoating began quite

---

[1] From "Ah, Holy Jesus" translated by Robert S. Bridges. From *The Yattendon Hymnal.* Used by permission of Oxford University Press.

early, for it is found in the New Testament. The Gospel of Matthew is especially anti-Semitic. Its diatribes against the Pharisees and its exclusive transcript of the trial before Pilate are all suspect. Matthew's account has the mob deliberately say, "His blood be on us, and on our children." Of course, we can understand the early Christian hostility toward the Jews, because at that time the Jews were excommunicating and persecuting the Christians right and left. This explains, but doesn't excuse, the anti-Semitism in the New Testament. But this New Testament anti-Semitism tends to perpetuate itself.

When the Oberammergau Passion Play resumed its tenth-yearly presentation of the gospel crucifixion story we heard the charges of anti-Semitism raised again. Just recently Jews circulated extensive criticism of *Jesus Christ Superstar* on the same grounds. What Jews resent here is the labeling of Jews in general as the villains in the Christ story.

With the Nazi holocaust less than thirty years past, we should be able to understand why Jews are sensitive. Adolf Hitler said, "I believe that I am acting in accordance with the will of the Almighty Creator: by defending myself against the Jew I am fighting for the work of the Lord." Where in Europe did that crazy little Austrian paperhanger with a Roman Catholic background ever get such a religious belief against the Jews? Just over a decade ago, in 1959, there was an outbreak of violence and vandalism against Jews in Europe and America—643 incidents in the United States alone. How can we explain the persistence of anti-Semitism among youth reared and educated in anti-Nazi postwar America? Could its source be the latent anti-Semitism in Christian teaching itself? On behalf of the Anti-Defamation League, two University of California sociologists, Charles Glock and Rodney Stark, conducted a random survey of the religious beliefs and racial attitudes of ninety-seven Protestant and twenty-one Catholic congregations in the San Francisco area. Comparison of this California sample with personal interviews across the country seems to indicate a religious basis for prejudice against Jews in America. The findings seem to indicate that the more liberal Christian bodies, including the Methodists and Congregationalists, are considerably less biased than the more conservative ones such as the Southern Baptists and the Missouri Lutherans. But all Christians show a disturbing degree of bias.

Sammy Davis Jr.'s appearance on "All in the Family" was quite an event. Arch-WASP Archie Bunker had a difficult time entertaining in his own home a celebrity who was both black and Jewish. Sammy Davis Jr. used to joke about his background, "My mother is Puerto Rican, my father is colored, my wife is Swedish, and I'm Jewish. Man, there ain't too many neighborhoods I can move into."

Fortunately the decade of the sixties saw considerable progress in Jewish-Christian relations. The Second Vatican Council's 1965 *Declaration on the Relationship of the Church to Non-Christian Religions* made a remarkable change in emphasis. The Vatican document insisted, first, that the origin of Christianity within Judaism gives the Christian church a special and intimate relationship to the People of the Book, as to a parent, and that both share a common hope for heaven and the kingdom of God; second, that the crucifixion of Christ is not to be blamed on the Jews as a people or in any way on Jews living today, nor are Jews to be considered as a cursed race because they did not accept Christ as their Messiah; third, that all forms of anti-Semitism are expressly repudiated by the Council as unchristian and unwarranted.

Parent and Child

Not only must we eliminate any possible basis for bigotry in our Christian teaching, but we Christians must realize how very important Judaism is for Christianity. Romans 9–11 illustrates this parent-child relationship with Paul's image of the olive tree. Picture a beautiful, bountiful olive tree centuries old. This represents Israel, the people of God, chosen for mission to humanity. The tree has deep roots approximately thirty-five hundred years old in the soil of God's saving action in history. Our roots go down deeper than John Wesley in the eighteenth century or Martin Luther in the sixteenth century or Jesus in the first century. Our roots plunge down to the patriarchs of faith, to Abraham, Isaac, and Jacob, fifteen hundred years before Jesus of Nazareth. Now, says Paul, we Gentiles who have become Christians are like branches broken off a wild olive tree and grafted onto the cultivated olive tree of Israel. Not all the branches of Israel have stayed on the tree. But there is a true stock of the people of God. One of these days, after all the wild branches of the Gentile Christians are grafted, the broken Jewish branches will be added. The Jews will finally be saved, and God's Israel will come to its full and intended growth.

Christian Rapprochement with Judaism

Now if we agree with Paul that God has not abandoned the Jews, that their blindness to Christ is temporary and we are to share with them in the consummation of God's redemptive purpose for mankind, then we are going to have to take Judaism more seriously.

Let us start with the Old Testament. Our neglect of the Old Testament shows up in our faulty impressions. Some years ago Dr. Francis Wayland was speaking to a class at Brown University and praised the Proverbs of the Old Testament. A supercilious student interrupted to say that he didn't think much of the Proverbs—"They are rather commonplace remarks of common people." "All right," said Wayland; "make *one*." The Old Testament has often been mistakenly characterized by Christians as expressing a religion of wrath. You hear that quite often even from ministers who should know better. The Old Testament speaks of a God of wrath and law, while the New Testament speaks of grace and love, they say. Yet the Old Testament prophet Hosea likens God to an injured husband who takes back his prostitute wife (Israel) again and again. Why? Because he loves her. That is why a Christian could write a book entitled *The Cross in Hosea*. He could do the same for Isaiah and Jeremiah. This is precisely why the New

Testament writers quote extensively from the Hebrew Scriptures to legitimate their claim that Christ is the completion not the deletion of Israel.

The Old and New Testaments belong together. They cannot be separated. A fluttery society lady, seated between a bishop and a rabbi at a banquet, said with affected coyness: "I feel as though I were a leaf between the Old Testament and the New Testament." "That page," said the bishop sourly, "is usually blank." We have too many blank pages between our Old and New Testaments. We Christians are going to have to take our Jewish heritage more seriously.

This also means taking seriously Judaism since the Old Testament. There has been a blank page between Christianity and Judaism since they went their separate ways in the first century of the Common Era. We need to acknowledge God's revelation of and witness to himself in both Judaism and Christianity, without denying the irreducible differences which do exist. Then we can begin our dialogue in earnest. As children we want to honor our father and mother, Judaism, even as we love our brothers and sisters in Christ.

Christ Uncompromised

As Christians we must also insist that Jews hear what we are saying and becoming when we present Jesus Christ. E. Stanley Jones tells of addressing a Jewish group on the significance of Christianity. He vigorously stressed the centrality of Christ. After his lecture was over, a rabbi came up to him. Jones asked, "Was I too Christian for you?" "No," said the rabbi, "the more Christian you are the better you treat the Jews." What you do speaks so loud I can't hear what you say. These are two important aspects of our witness—speaking and doing.

One of the great episodes in Jewish history—our history—was when Moses returned from the mountaintop with the tables of the law from God, only to find the people left below worshiping a golden calf. Moses was angry. God was angry. But Moses pleaded for his people that they might be forgiven; but if not, says Moses, blot me out of the book of life as well. Paul recalls this instance in Romans 9 when he says he is willing to be cursed by God and cut off from Christ if that could in any way bring his Jewish people to the Lord Jesus. Do we really love Jews and those of other religions deeply enough, with the love of Christ in our hearts, to want them to be saved—saved even at our own expense if necessary?

When a son or daughter has done something wrong and brought suffering upon himself or herself, many fathers and mothers would gladly bear that suffering if only they could. The black school principal who shot himself in a Detroit suburb addressed his suicide note to the black kids who were more interested in making trouble than in making progress. He said, "I die for you." A man looking down from the top of the Empire State Building in New York, seeing the people like gnats on the pavement 102 floors below, said, "That is how the world must look to God." The early Christians, however, gave a different view: "Greater love hath no man than this, that a man lay down his life for his friends"; "God so loved the world, that he gave his only begotten Son, that whosoever believeth in him should not perish, but have everlasting life."

Christians are not in the business of proclaiming the superiority of the Christian church. We are signposts, direction signals, witnesses. Pointing toward Christ with the Evangelist of John Bunyan's *Pilgrim's Progress*, we say to all, "Keep that Light in your eye, and go directly thereto, so thou shalt see the Gate."

A Revolution for Religions

Paul sees the Jews as necessary members of the household of God to be completed in the future, and their religion as a preparation for the gospel. This viewpoint can be applied to other faiths as well. Paul's knowledge of other religions was limited. But he was convinced that the Holy Spirit does work among the pagans (those of other religions) to bring them to Christ. Our studies of other religions will reveal the ways in which they too are preparations for the gospel of Jesus Christ.

Such a position will not be acceptable to non-Christians. Rabbi Levi Olan rejects any such subordination of Judaism as a faith which must come to Christ for fulfillment. He prefers to speak of Judaism and Christianity as two irreconcilable, contradictory faiths.[2] Thus a Reformed rabbi speaks very much like a Protestant

[2] Levi Olan, "Christian-Jewish Dialogue: A Dissenting Opinion," *Religion in Life*, Summer, 1972, pp. 154-78.

fundamentalist. It is true that we should not ask each other to scrap our uniqueness in order to accommodate one another—to achieve some flat-bladed religion of the lowest common denominator. The sharp, single cutting edge is essential for vitality in any faith.

But if our function as Christians is to point away from ourselves and our institutions toward Christ, to see his preparing Spirit at work in every corner of the earth in every humanizing faith and way, then we must become far more open to the other religions of mankind. We will become listeners, sharers, sufferers, as well as witnesses convinced that the Light of the World cannot be hid no matter how big our bushel baskets. Christ is the Omega point at the end of history who will bring us together. Ecumenism is a much bigger word, a far more revolutionary concept, than we Christians first thought.

6 What the Church Needs Now

Romans 12—15

"I appeal to you therefore, brethren, by the mercies of God, to present your bodies as a living sacrifice, holy and acceptable to God, which is your spiritual worship. Do not be conformed to this world but be transformed by the renewal of your mind, that you may prove what is the will of God, what is good and acceptable and perfect" (Romans 12:1-2 RSV).

"I" Trouble

I appeal to you—but who am I to beseech you? I am a sinner. I swear and sweat, I boast and complain. I put one pant leg on at a time. I get confused and caught between my ideals and my compromises. I'll end up in a casket and I don't know the day or the hour. Why should I dare prescribe any way of life for you, since I'm in the same boat you are?

A party to a lawsuit had to return home before the jury had brought in its verdict. When the case was decided in his favor, his lawyer wired him: Right and justice won. To which the client replied, Appeal at once. A legal appeal can be made regardless of right and justice—but not a moral appeal. On what grounds can a white man make a moral appeal to an Indian or a Negro? What gives George Wallace the right to appeal to Americans for brotherhood, or President Nixon the basis for asking our trust in his administration? What gives any of us the right? We have all deceived our brothers and sisters even in our own families; we have all lied through our teeth; we have all praised the Lord on Sunday and crucified him on Friday. What gives you the right to tell me how to run my life? That's a very good question. Yeah!

> Jesus, White Boy, holding out your hand,
> Can you ever really understand?
> I can't shake your hand, it isn't right;
> I'm too black and you're too lily white.
>
> Black is what men use to label dirt;
> Then expect us all to be unhurt.
> If you love us all, as we have heard,
> You have got to find another word.
>
> Sin is black and night and evil too;
> Jesus, White Boy, what are we to do?
> If I take your white hand with my black,
> Will you help me up, or hold me back? [1]

I appeal to you, therefore, brethren and sisters, by the mercies of God. Thomas Aquinas once said to Bonaventura, "Show me your library." Bonaventura took

[1] "Jesus, White Boy." Copyright 1967 by Richard K. Avery and Donald S. Marsh (ASCAP) from *Hymns Hot and Carols Cool*. All rights reserved. Used by permission of Proclamation Productions, Inc., Orange Square, Port Jervis, N.Y. 12771.

Thomas Aquinas to his cell and pointed to a crucifix before which he prayed. "There it is," he said. There is the whole library of God's mercies—Jesus Christ the Crucified.

A conversation was heard in a dugout in World War I: "Here, Dominique, take my papers with you. I'm dying and have no need of them. You have a bad reputation and a police record—I'm clean. Take my identity and I'll take yours. You can have a new beginning." Do you hear the voice of Christ there, the mercies of God?

> There's a wideness in God's mercy,
>   Like the wideness of the sea;
> There's a kindness in his justice,
>   Which is more than liberty.
> There is welcome for the sinner,
>   And more graces for the good;
> There is mercy with the Savior;
>   There is healing in his blood.
>
> For the love of God is broader
>   Than the measure of man's mind;
> And the heart of the Eternal
>   Is most wonderfully kind.

St. Paul cataloged these mercies of God in Romans 1–11. Then comes that mighty *therefore,* the inevitable one-way bridge from God across the chasm of this world's ambiguities to us. There it is, the Royal Gorge of emptiness and nothing, an abyss of the absurd right down the middle of your life and mine: the bikini-clad beauty who shrivels up into a toothless old hag; the crumbling tombs of pharaohs and presidents; the strong eating the weak; the rich saying, "I don't have a dime to spare" to the poor; the certainty of death to physician, prince, and pauper alike. But by his mercy God bridges that awful chasm, comes over to our side, takes our inhumanity into his humanity, our hurt into his healing, our evil into his good, our hate into his love. *Therefore,* on the basis of, in consequence of, the mercies of God—*I appeal to you.*

The Behaving Side

I appeal to you to behave like a Christian. "The gospel has two sides," the old preacher said; "a believing side and a behaving side." After many chapters of Romans, Paul says, "I appeal to you by God's mercies to behave like a Christian. Present your bodies as a living sacrifice, holy and acceptable to God which is your spiritual worship."

Have you seen the altars of human sacrifice in the old Aztec ruins outside Mexico City; the sacred Mayan well of human sacrifice in Yucatan? A newlywed husband was heard to say, "My wife worships me. At every meal she offers burnt sacrifices." Humanity is forever sacrificing its youth to Mammon and Mars like an ancient Abraham willing to give up his son Isaac. But St. Paul asks that we present our bodies, not as a dying sacrifice, but as a living one to be offered constantly in the temples of industry and commerce, in the sanctuaries of daily decision—the home, the school, the gym, the courthouse.

The Rev. William E. Crews, an Episcopal minister, conducts what he calls a "lobby for God" as chaplain of New Mexico's House of Representatives. Some of his prayers have drawn protests from legislators and occasional suggestion that they be referred to committee: "Almighty God, we politicians are like pianos: grand, square, upright, but of no eternal use unless we are attuned to your will and have the courage to put it into action"; "Present your bodies a living sacrifice, holy and acceptable to God." Here is another lobby for God by Chaplain Crews: "Almighty God, who has given us the ability to reason our problems, grant us the courage to vote as we have reasoned. Forgive the animosity of the majority when we stand in the minority and let us never presume to equate numbers of votes with the will of God. We ask this in the name of one who never won a committee vote nor was ever found among the majority opinion of his day."

Squeezed in the World's Mold

What is this living sacrifice of our total life to God? Is this not love for our neighbor, the sacrifice of self for others? *"Be not conformed to this world,"* exhorts St. Paul. Certainly Christlike caring does not conform to this world. It is about as alien, strange, miraculous, and impossible a commodity as is imaginable in our world. Here is St. Paul's description of Christlike caring in Romans: "I bid everyone among you not to think of himself more highly than he ought to think. . . . Bless those who persecute you. . . . Live in harmony with one another; do not be haughty, but associate with the lowly;

never be conceited. Repay no one evil for evil, but take thought for what is noble in the sight of all. . . . Never avenge yourselves, but leave it to the wrath of God. . . . If your enemy is hungry, feed him; if he is thirsty, give him drink. . . . Do not be overcome by evil, but overcome evil with good. . . . Love your neighbor as yourself. . . . Love is the fulfilling of the law" (Romans 12:3–13:10 RSV).

Someone has contrasted heaven and hell by imagining them set up in the same way, with all their citizens seated around a great banquet table, their hands shackled to it. In hell the emaciated guests at God's table are starving because all they are concerned about is feeding themselves and their shackled hands won't reach. By contrast, in heaven at God's gracious table the citizens are full and happy because each person has discovered that his shackled hands will reach to feed his neighbor. All have enough, for each is caring for the other. Whenever you see that kind of love you see a miracle, you see God, you see a creative and saving possibility in every situation.

Renewal Can Spell Revolution

"Be not conformed to this world, but be transformed by the renewal of your mind." Dietrich Bonhoeffer spoke of obedience being the essence of faith. Jesus' call to follow is a call to come and die—die to self-love so that the self may really begin to live and love in Christ. And Bonhoeffer forgot himself, took up his cross in the

church-state struggle of Nazi Germany, and followed Christ.

Bonhoeffer was a young German theologian of the Nazi era who went underground with the Confessing Church in Germany. By Confessing Church I mean that small church which through resistance and civil disobedience stood up against the Nazi takeover of the Lutheran state church. The outspoken pastors went to jail. The faithful congregations had their water, lights, and heat turned off and their food stamps stopped. Seminaries for training young pastors went underground, and Bonhoeffer went with them to teach these young pastors-in-training. He had not yet been caught and thrown into prison but he lived in constant danger.

In 1939 Reinhold Niebuhr and other friends arranged for Bonhoeffer to teach at Union Theological Seminary in New York City. Paul Tillich and Richard Kroner too had gotten out to safety to continue their teaching. This was certainly one valid option in continuing witness for Christ. Albert Einstein and a number of other German scholars had also been given asylum in America.

Wernher von Braun stayed in Germany to develop long-range rockets which delivered their cargo of death to London, until he chose at the end of the war to surrender to the Americans rather than the Russians. And instead of being tried as a war criminal at Nuremberg he was embraced by the American military-industrial complex and went on to build our missiles and direct NASA's Marshall Space Flight Center. These were some of the options for German intellectuals.

Bonhoeffer stayed in the safety of New York City for

only a few months, and then, despite his friends' urging, he went back to Germany just before war broke out. He believed his place was with his own people in suffering with the Confessing Church under persecution. "The Son of man must suffer much. . . . If anyone wants to come with me he must forget himself, take up his cross every day and follow me." "Come and Die."

Then when Bonhoeffer heard what his country was doing to the Jews and to some protesting Christians, his politics took a more radical turn. He joined a group which tried and failed to assassinate the Fuehrer. Obedience to Christ in that demonic situation led him to violent opposition. He was caught and punished by imprisonment and death. And today his memory is an embarrassment to all the German Christians who went along with Hitler—whose shallow patriotism and religion taught them no more than reverent obedience to a demonic state. These Germans want to claim that Bonhoeffer was executed as a political rebel. But Bonhoeffer believed that his political actions were an unmistakable obedience to the suffering Savior, in not conforming to the world but being transformed by Christ. He risked all for the sake of his fellows because of Christ.

Transformation, not *conformation*. The transformer is the mind of God. Plug into the transcendental consciousness. Get a new mind, a new viewpoint; hold onto that impossible possibility, that Christ the crucified is King, that God is self-sacrificing love, that God loves you and you can love others, that death is swallowed up in victory.

Palm Sunday in the church year is always a parable of the church's credibility gap:

> They pluck their palm branches and hail him as King,
>   Early on Sunday;
> They spread out their garments; hosannas they sing,
>   Early on Sunday.
>
> But where is the noise of their hurrying feet,
>   The crown they would offer, the scepter, the seat?
> Their King wanders hungry, forgot in the street,
>   Early on Monday.[2]

Someone has written: "When I think of the church as Christians who sing praise to God on Sunday but who have no inclination to let Monday's work be a hymn of praise to God. I am fearful for the church.

"When I think of the church as Christians who go to church on Sunday, but could not prove it for all the compassion they show toward the oppressed and forgotten poor, I am fearful for the church.

"When I think of the church as Christians whose fine prayers are shot so full of hypocrisy because they pray for the needy but reinforce the values that imprison the needy, I am fearful for the church.

"When I think of the church as Christians whose respectability will not permit them to take risks for those who are less respectable than they are, I am fearful for the church.

"I am fearful for the church because I know how easy it is for me to be such a Christian, and therefore I know how easy it is for you to be such a Christian."

[2] "Palm Sunday and Monday" from *Over the Sea the Sky* by Edwin McNeill Poteat. Copyright 1945 by Harper & Row, Publishers, Inc. Reprinted by permission of the publishers.

What the church needs now is love, sweet love—behaving as well as believing, morality as well as meaning, living portrayal in the streets as well as loud praise and glad hosannas.

Is that revolting or revolutionary?

> In this world of napalm cremations,
> In this world of sad assassinations,
> There will be some changes made.
> I hear a distant drumming,
> It's signaling they're coming.
> Love is on the way.
>
> In a world where all kinds of movements
> Scream their selfish program of improvements,
> There will be some changes made.
> The drums are here behind us
> And ready to remind us
> Love is on the way.
>
> Cry aloud the great proclamation.
> Join the cause of love and liberation.
> There will be some changes made.
> We're ready to be led now,
> The drums are up ahead now;
> Love is on the way.
>
> Come on and join the revolution,
> Join the revolution!
> Get the action started where you are.
> Start the boulders rolling.
> Start the church bells tolling.
> God is alive and marching, marching, marching!
> A revolution's going on, the resurrection began
> at dawn.[3]

[3] "Join the Revolution." Copyright 1970 by Richard K. Avery and Donald S. Marsh (ASCAP) from *More, More, More*. All rights reserved. Used by permission of Proclamation Productions, Inc., Orange Square, Port Jervis, N.Y. 12771.

7 Overflowing with Hope

Romans 15—16

A Way Out?

Tick, tick, tick, tick—listen to the sound of your watch. Perhaps yours runs slower—tick, tock, tick, tock—like the beating th-dum, th-dum, th-dum of your heart. Someday that tick, tick, tick, that th-dum, th-dum, th-dum, will stop. Our time will run out. Our hearts will fail. We hope we can get new works for the watch. We hope for a heart transplant, for a pacemaker, for some new medical discovery to prolong our lives. Give to the heart fund. Support cancer research. Until we breathe our last we hope for a miracle: "Hope springs eternal in the human breast." When George Frederick Watts painted *Hope,* he drew her as a battered, bowed figure with only one string left on her lyre.

Every farmer who waits for the seed to sprout, the rain to fall, the sun to shine; every mother who waits and waits for the life within her to be born; every truly active person who waits for his project to bear fruit; every suffering person who waits for healing to take place, knows that we live on hope. "Give me your tired, your poor, your huddled masses yearning to breathe free," said the lady of hope in New York's harbor to Europe's forgotten multitudes. And they came—Germans, Italians, Jews, Poles—lured by the hope of a new world, a new beginning. In the garden of the United Nations in New York City there is a giant sculpture representing humanity beating its sword into a plowshare, the vision of Isaiah, a gift of the USSR—a hope for peace among all peoples, of which the United Nations is the greatest expression. We live on hope, Don Quixotes challenging the principalities and powers of this world with an impossible dream.

But sooner or later the tick, tick, tick, th-dum, th-dum, th-dum, will stop. Our human hopes are limited at best. Some of the immigrants hoping for a better life in America wound up appealing to the Godfather for hoodlum justice. And the tragic irony of a Jewish prophet's dream for peace sculpted by the Russians and erected in an American peace garden is too obvious to require comment. Recently I previewed a "Religion in American Life" television spot which illustrated this anguished "Yes" and "No" of human existence. It showed a young couple strolling hand in hand in the park, and next the rapid-fire explosions of a machine gun in darkened city streets. It showed a circle of kids playing a game, and a little spastic girl trying her best to run. It showed a beautiful Easter dinner with the family gathered all around in a very nice home, and next a tired old woman sitting on her sleazy cot in a tenement room. It showed a dancing waterfall framed in green, and then a filth-strewn stream in someone's backyard Appalachia. It showed a countdown at Cape Kennedy, and the rapid departure from this blue planet for the moon.

"Is there any hope, Doctor?" asked the patient's wife.

"It all depends upon what you're hoping for," replied the doctor. He's right. The body-doctor cannot promise you freedom from death. The head-doctor cannot promise you freedom from worry. The soul-doctor cannot promise you freedom from sin. The community-doctor cannot promise you universal peace and brotherhood. We hope for such freedoms and work for such liberation. But such hopes can never be fully realized within the tick, tick, tick, th-dum, th-dum, th-dum of our lifetime.

The French atheist-existentialist Jean-Paul Sartre wrote a play entitled *No Exit,* which showed how human beings are locked into a room with each other from which there is no way out. We hope for a way out. In the sciences, the arts, and morality we search for a way out. Once in a while we discover some new sciences, a new art, and a new morality, but we still find ourselves locked in with no exit. We sin and suffer, and all our yesterdays are a pile of shattered utopias—New Harmony, Indiana, or the Democratic People's Republics of the Eastern world. We all live at the cross. The tragedy of Good Friday is our tragedy. Calvary's "No" to the finest "Yes" of human life is our human misery and despair. Once we realize this we can begin to hope in God.

A Benediction of Hope

We have God's word to us through St. Paul's Epistle to the Romans, from Paul the pessimist about human sin in this hell of a world. Toward the end of his theological treatise Paul gives us a benediction of hope: "May the God of hope fill you with all joy and peace by your faith in him, until, by the power of the Holy Spirit, you overflow with hope" (Romans 15:13 NEB). We should have seen it coming, because we learned in the first chapter of Romans that Paul's God is a God of resurrection, a God who takes the dregs of despair and starts anew, a God who takes the crucifixion of Jesus by sinful men and turns it into a victory.

One of the great American novels of the twentieth century is William Faulkner's *The Sound and the Fury*. Here we see the suffering of the Compson family, and each family member's reaction to that suffering. Mr. Compson deadens his pain with cynicism and whiskey. Mrs. Compson is a self-pitying hypochondriac. Jason Compson wears a coat of callous indifference; his brother Quentin commits suicide; sister Candace can't be counted on for anything; and poor idiot Benjy is oblivious to all. Only Dilsy, the black maid and mammy to the family, stands up to the sound and fury of life with tenderness and courage. She alone prevents them from collapsing completely. She endures as have other Dilsys of this world. And the secret of their endurance? Dilsy sees her secret in the proclamation of the Christian gospel, in an Easter sermon by a black preacher from St. Louis. Here is the promise that gives her hope and sustains the large spirit in her tired and worn body: "I see de resurrection en de light; sees de meek Jesus saying, 'Dey kilt me dat ye shall live again; I died dat dem what sees and believes shall never die.' Breddren, O breddren! I sees de doom crack and hears de golden horns shoutin down de glory, and de arisen dead what got de blood and de religion of de lamb."

Christianity is a religion of resurrection, of a God who continually breaks into our exitless room and opens the door to new possibilities. When our hopes run out at Good Friday there is the God of hope standing beside the empty tomb, standing by the bed of our chronically ill, standing by us when we goof up and goof off bringing suffering upon ourselves and others, standing by us when life closes in and the bottom falls out. One of the great Christian creeds affirms: I believe in God; I believe in Jesus Christ; I believe in the Holy Spirit; I believe in the communion of saints; I believe in the life everlasting. It all goes together—belief in a God of hope who gives us hope now and hope beyond the boundary of human hopes.

The God of Hope

The God of hope tells us there are no hopeless persons. I've heard people say of themselves, "I'm hopeless. You might as well give up on me." Or we say that of others, and institutionalize such an attitude when we lock persons in a prison with no funds, no programs, no staff to rehabilitate. But if we believe in the God of resurrection, the God of hope, there are no hopeless persons. There is a possibility for change, renewal, resurrection in every human being. We are not chained to the wheel of Karma, an endless, hopeless repetition of yesterdays, reaping what we have sown, lying in the bed we have made for ourselves. No; as the God of hope lives there is a way out—repentance, change of heart and mind, forgiveness, and new beginnings and endings.

In the beautiful, striped marble baptistry of Florence, Italy, just across the street from the cathedral, there is a wonderful statue of Mary Magdalene, the prostitute. She is portrayed as a gaunt, degraded hag; but her head is lifted up, and in her eyes the carver has placed an extraordinary if desperate hope. It is the moment when she discovers the Savior. One can almost hear her whisper: "There is life for me. That is what I can become." We are saved by the hope Christ sets before us. The old woman put it beautifully: "I know I ain't what I ought to be, but thank God almighty, I ain't always going to be what I am." There are no hopeless persons.

With the God of hope there are no hopeless situations. We wonder about those pregnant young women in Bangladesh, raped by enemy soldiers, and then unwanted by their Moslem husbands and fiancés. There was some talk of shipping them to another country. Is theirs a hopeless situation? Does history face us with situations which have no rational, no compassionate solution, as if the stuff of history itself were absurd? Someone has said there are no hopeless situations, only hopeless people.

There is a story about a British cabinet meeting in the darkest days of World War II just after the fall of France. Mr. Churchill, not yet prime minister, outlined the situation in its starkest colors. Quite literally, Britain stood alone, ripe for invasion. There was a silence when he had finished speaking, and on the faces of some there

was written despair, and there were some who would
have given up the struggle. Churchill was silent for a
moment; then he looked around that dispirited company. "Gentlemen," he said, "I find it rather inspiring."
The God of resurrection, the God of hope, gives every
situation, no matter how discouraging, the possibility
of a creative solution.

With the God of hope this is not a hopeless universe.
H. G. Wells once said, "Man, who began in a cave
behind a windbreak, will end in the disease-soaked
ruins of a slum." Not so St. Paul. He saw man's sin and
the deplorable state of the world; but he also saw God's
redeeming power, and in the end, for Paul, there was
hope. He saw a whole universe groaning and travailing
like a woman in childbirth, reaching for new life—a
liberation, a renovation, a re-creation, a resurrection,
wrought by the glory and the power of the God of hope.
This planet may pull away from the sun and become a
frozen graveyard or be drawn into the sun to become a
hot cinder. It is possible that evil men could snuff out
human life with hydrogen bombs: all of us cremated
equal. But beyond this materialistic part of our existence
—the "bread alone" we say we cannot live by—God
has plans for our personal life beyond the grave, everlasting life; plans for the corporate rejuvenation of
humanity, the kingdom of God; plans for the ultimate
vindication of his loving purpose in all of creation, the
final judgment.

Franz Schubert, dying at thirty-one and leaving behind his "Unfinished" Symphony, is a symbol of every
person, every situation, in this whole universe. This tick,
tick, tick, th-dum, th-dum, th-dum, of all creation will

end. But with the God of hope there are no unfinished symphonies. Anything he starts he will finish. Focus your energies on the coming new day. Turn your mortal tick, tick, th-dum, th-dum, into a two-step with the Lord of the Dance:

I danced in the morning when the world was begun
And I danced in the moon and the stars and the sun,
And I came down from heaven and I danced on the earth.
At Bethlehem I had my birth.

I danced for the scribe and the pharisee,
But they would not dance and they would not follow me.
I danced for the fishermen, for James and John;
They came to me and the dance went on.

I danced on the Sabbath and I cured the lame,
The holy people said it was a shame;
They whipped and they stripped and they hung me high,
And they left me there on a cross to die.

I danced on a Friday when the sky turned black.
It's hard to dance with the devil on your back.
They buried my body and they thought I'd gone,
But I am the dance and I still go on.

They cut me down and I leapt up high,
I am the life that'll never, never die;
I'll live in you if you live in me.
I am the Lord of the Dance, said he.

Refrain: Dance, then, wherever you may be;
I am the Lord of the Dance, said he,
And I'll lead you all wherever you may be,
And I'll lead you all in the dance, said he.[1]

[1] "Lord of the Dance" by Sydney Carter. Copyright © 1963 by Galliard Ltd. All rights reserved. Used by permission of Galaxy Music Corp., N.Y., sole U.S. agent.

Part II
Historical Variations on the Themes of Romans

It has been Paul's historic work across the centuries to turn men back to the Lord into whose service he had unreservedly committed himself. And today too, Paul still fulfills this task for everyone who is ready to listen to his message, whether we meet him with theological questions, or simply with seeking hearts.

Martin Dibelius

8 Great Lion of God

For he was a veritable lion, a red lion, the great lion of God.

—St. Augustine

A servant of Jesus Christ, and an apostle chosen and called by God to preach his Good News.

—Romans 1:1 (TEV)

What a remarkable man, and what great accomplishments were his during twenty-five years of ministry. Born in the seaport and university city of Tarsus in Asia Minor, Paul was reared in a Greek-speaking family of Jews, in one of many Jewish immigrant colonies scattered throughout the Mediterranean world. In his letters Paul tells us that he grew up to be a most rigorous Pharisee, a Jewish fanatic who led the persecution of the Christian cult. But conversion by God turned him from a Jewish gestapo agent hounding Christians into a Christian missionary trying to win the world for Christ.

In her novel *Great Lion of God,* Taylor Caldwell portrays Paul as an angry young man intent on perfection for himself and everyone else. But Caldwell's Paul reflects her own resistance to change in the Roman Catholic Church and the modern world. She is attached to the past, where as the real St. Paul was a revolutionary, cutting loose from the past and pioneering into the future.

From Judaism to Christianity

The real St. Paul was a liberator. Like Charles de Gaulle and the Free French forces liberating Paris on March 25, 1945, Paul marched into Jerusalem and liberated Christianity from Judaism. Any catalog of the great battles of the world would include Marathon, Issus, Hastings, Gettysburg, the Normandy Landings, and Guadalcanal. But what about Paul's battle with the Jewish Christians in Jerusalem? That changed the course of history decisively.

The year is A.D. 48 in the month of June; the place—First Church, Jerusalem; the occasion—the most important church conference in the history of Christianity. The issue: whether you and I should have to become practicing Jews before we can be recognized as true Christians. The principals: Paul, Barnabas, Titus (a Greek convert of Paul), against Peter, James, and John, leaders of the Jerusalem Church.

The church in Jerusalem was trying to be faithful to the Mosaic law, observing the rituals, keeping the food taboos, practicing the rite of circumcision, and worshiping at the temple services. Like Judaism it was narrow, legalistic, and exclusive of Gentiles. On the other hand, St. Paul, having worked among the Gentiles for fourteen years since his conversion, was convinced that the Holy Spirit was leading them to Christ, and was establishing churches among them through his ministry. Now some of the Jewish Christians were wanting all Gentile Christians to be circumcised and were questioning his authority as a preacher. So the lion roared into Jerusalem to have it out. The argument was a hot one. Some of the Jewish Christians insisted that Titus, the Greek convert, be circumcised or else sent away from the church meeting. "Never," retorted Paul. "We will hold our ground and use Titus as our example. They argue that a person must be a Jew to be a Christian. That ties the gospel to one nation. It does not offer good news to persons as persons, but only to persons as Jews. It implies that to become a Jew is superior to faith in Jesus Christ. That is to be false to the gospel. Titus is not a Jew yet he believes in Jesus. He is a worthy Christian. This demonstrates that Judaism can add nothing to Christianity and that the gospel is free to go to the whole world without the restrictions of Judaism."

The lion roared and the Jerusalem church conceded. Christianity turned with the apostle Paul toward the whole world, with Jesus Christ rather than the Jewish law as its center. What about us today? Are we hung up on the unessentials of the past—familiar routines of worship and witness, the way we have always done it, a race and sex discrimination in appointment to ministry within the church? Churchmen like to think of themselves as spokesmen for peace and harmony, but then are often inactive in the political fight for justice and responsibility. Paul fought the injustice of the Jewish Christians who were refusing to have table fellowship with Gentile Christians. How close this is to the fight in our day for table fellowship between blacks and whites, altar fellowship between Lutherans and Lutherans, between Methodists and Catholics! The lion still roars from the letters of the New Testament. Where do we go from here?

From Moralism to Faith

The apostle Paul liberated the Christian faith from moralism. By moralism, I mean the command to be good, to work for justice, to love your neighbor, without any help in doing so. Moralism would whip up our human weakness to do what we "ought" to do. It is preoccupied with doing rather than becoming. It senses no need of forgiveness for the past; no need for godly power to bring moral change.

The Judaizers in Paul's day and our own are quite willing to take Jesus the teacher and Jesus the rebel as their moral standard. Jesus becomes the new law. The imitation of Christ, walking in his steps, doing what he would do, following the religion of Jesus, is an old and ever new option. The present-day portrayal of Jesus as "The Man," the rebel against the temple establishment and Roman oppression, the Superstar so appealing to many young people, may be no more than just the old moralism—Be a good boy or girl by following the greatest man who ever lived. And certainly there could be no better life to follow.

Together magazine carried a feature interview with a typical middle-American churchgoing family, which happened to be a family chosen from my congregation in the Midwest. When they were asked to spell out the meaning, to them, of the Christian faith, it came out very moralistic. Being a Christian amounted to going to church, saying your prayers, and trying hard to follow Jesus. The mother then admitted how very frustrating this kind of "strain-to-be-perfect life" can be.

Turning to St. Paul we find a completely different emphasis. It was not the example of Jesus' earthly life that gripped the attention of Paul and most of the early church. Of his miracles Paul breathes hardly a word. Of his teachings Paul gives few direct quotations. To incidents in the Carpenter's life he scarcely refers. Anecdotes about the Nazarene he rarely relates. It is the cross and the empty tomb that hold Paul's gaze and inspire his devotion. Who is this one who forgave sinners, identified with tax collectors and drunkards, who submitted to the cross and was resurrected from the dead? The only possible answer for Paul was God, God in Christ making friends of sinful men and women who have faith in him—not only the religion of Jesus, but the religion about Jesus as well. The new Adam has come to turn mankind around: "If any one is in Christ, he is a new creation; the old has passed away, behold, the new has come" (II Corinthians 5:17 RSV). God has come in Christ to enable us to become children of God and bring his kingdom on earth as it is in heaven.

As we knock about this tired old planet with one life to live, we Christians have something more to say to mankind than "Pick up your courage and try harder, buddy." We have good news of a God who loves us so much that he enters into our frail, faulty human life to accept us as we are and help us to be better. We have good news for that father with cancer and that young girl in jail who has tried everything, for that self-sufficient salesman and that politician in high office who think they can hustle anything and anybody until old age and depression set in.

A prodigal son, very much ashamed of the harm and hurt he had done to his parents, wrote home to effect a reconciliation. He was sorry for what he had done and hoped he could come home and make good. He would be coming into town on the train which passed the homeplace. "Mom," he wrote, "tie a red rag on the tree in front of the house if you will accept me back. Then I'll know to get off at the station." On that day there was a very nervous young man sitting by the window as the train pulled into his hometown. He strained his eyes for his homeplace and the tree. When he saw it he broke into tears. There were red rags on every branch of the tree. Could it be Calvary's tree? St. Paul said God's love in Christ is like that for every prodigal one of us. Trust in him.

Thank God the lion still roars for faith in Christ against a shallow moralism.

From Libertinism to Responsibility

Paul also liberated Christian ethics from libertinism —"anything goes," "if it feels good do it," "doing what comes naturally." For with Paul's emphasis upon Christianity as living a life of faith in Christ rather than working our way to heaven merely by keeping the rules, there were opponents who charged him with being weak on morals and ethics—all faith and no works. Indeed, another epistle in the New Testament, that to James, makes this charge.

There was another crowd, this time in the church at Corinth, which really gave Paul fits. (Read I and II Corinthians, especially chapters 12, 13, and 14 of I Corinthians.) These were the Gnostics, the know-it-alls, who believed they had a special pipeline to heaven which relieved them of ethical responsibility to the rest of the church community. They didn't think anything of it when they broke up a worship service with a kind of gibberish jabbering of their own. They ate at bargain prices top sirloins left over from sacrificial offerings to pagan idols, although this disturbed the more conservative brethren. They patronized homosexuals and prostitutes in the accepted pagan manner—love without responsibility—because they were freed from moral restrictions. Morals didn't matter anyway to them: they were saved.

Well, the old lion roared and took up this battle as well. It is true that we are saved by grace through faith and not by following the Ten Commandments or the Golden Rule, Paul said. No law can bind the Christian: he is free. But then if we are in Christ we must try to act like it. We must yield ourselves to the Spirit of Christ so that our freedom does not degenerate into license. Paul illustrated this in his little postcard to

Philemon. While in jail at Ephesus, he became acquainted with a runaway slave by the name of Onesimus. Paul shared his faith with him, and Onesimus became a Christian. Now, as a Christian, should he continue to run from the master he had robbed and hurt? He felt an obligation to put things right according to the standards of that day. On the other hand, his owner, Philemon, was a Christian known to Paul. According to Roman law, the owner had every right to punish a runaway slave severely, even to take his life. But would the law prescribe the owner's full obligation to another human being?

Paul sent Onesimus home with this plea to Philemon: "Onesimus is not just a slave, but much more than a slave; he is a brother in Christ. If he has done you any wrong or owes you anything, charge it to my account." The love of Christ goes beyond the law but does not leave us free to do as we please; we are to do as Christ pleases in us and through us.

He's not heavy, Father; he's my brother. That's the Christian ethic as clarified by Paul. Today the law says that the hundred thousand young draft dodgers and deserters who decided earlier what most of us have now decided about the Vietnam war are too heavy for us to bear. But the Christian says; "They're not heavy, Father; they're my brothers." And the law says the poor man's hospital bill for his little girl's operation must be paid or the hospital will garnishee his wages and he will lose his job. But the Christian says, "I'll pay your bill and then we will both work for a better medical care system. You're not heavy, poor man. You're my brother."

The lion of God still roars from the letters of St. Paul: freedom, faith, responsibility in Christ.

Catalyst of Change

The highlight of the Air Force Academy at Colorado Springs is the beautiful chapel with its A-frame construction of exposed stainless steel triangles pointing heavenward. Actually there are three chapels there. The small Jewish chapel downstairs has as its focus, the Torah scrolls, the law of Moses so central to Judaism's walk with God. Close by is the Roman Catholic chapel, where the crucifix on the altar symbolizes Jesus Christ suffering for the sins of the whole world: "Behold, the Lamb of God, who takes away the sin of the world!" (John 1:29 RSV). Upstairs the Protestant chapel occupies the entire floor space under the soaring A-frames and faceted glass walls. Here the focus is upon an empty cross symbolizing the risen Lord present and available in all of life.

St. Paul marks each one of these transitions from Judaism to Roman Catholicism to Protestantism, roaring out the message and strategy of liberation. Where will this great lion of God lead us next? For the story of God's people has just begun.

9 The Warrior and His Weapons

"No orgies or drunkenness, no immorality or indecency, no fighting or jealousy. But take up the weapons of the Lord Jesus Christ, and stop giving attention to your sinful nature, to satisfy its desires."

These words of Romans 13:13–14 (TEV) will always be associated with the conversion of St. Augustine, in July, 386. There in the garden outside Milan, the intense struggle between his own bad habits and the Christian way of life came to a climax. Augustine had been looking at the Epistles of St. Paul and crying out in despair and hope, "How long, how long? Tomorrow and tomorrow? Why not now? Why should there not be an end to my uncleanness now?"

Then he heard a child's voice from another part of the garden, the singsong, repetitive game-playing of a child: *"Tolle, lege"* ("Take up and read"). The child was probably playing school and imitating the instructions of a teacher, but Augustine believed the words were from God. He ran to the Epistles of Paul and his eye fell on the words in the thirteenth chapter of Romans where St. Paul demands that the servant of Christ should renounce all voluptuous pleasures. You can't live like a James Bond and be a Christian—gambling, drinking, wenching, killing, "my country right or wrong": "no orgies or drunkenness, no immorality or indecency, no fighting or jealousy. But take up the weapons of the Lord Jesus Christ and stop giving attention to your sinful nature, to satisfy its desires."

Augustine put his finger in the page, calm at last, possessing a great peace. "There was infused in my heart something like the light of full certainty and all the gloom of doubt vanished away," he tells us. Thus at the age of thirty-two after many years of struggle, one of the most brilliant minds of Western civilization came to Christ. He is one of the most frequently quoted authors of the past (*E pluribus unum,* on the great seal of the United States, is from his pen). Augustine took the teachings of St. Paul, as stated in the Nicene Creed, and expounded and defended them for all later generations. Recognized as the Doctor of Grace by the medieval church, he was a great defender of the faith in a pluralistic society, an age of catastrophe.

Conversion of the Will

The primary barrier to Augustine's becoming a Christian was not intellectual; it was moral. His first conversion had to involve a change in his habits, his way of life. In his *Confessions* Augustine tells us of that struggle. He was born in Tagaste, North Africa, of a

Christian mother, Monica, and a pagan father. He received a Christian education, which he soon ignored. He became something of a teenage delinquent, stealing for the thrill of it, lying with abandon, and seducing the girls. At the University of Carthage, at the age of seventeen he took a mistress, and they had an illegitimate son the following year. For fifteen years Augustine was faithful to his mistress, although with tears and prayers his mother begged him to either get married or discontinue the relationship.

But Augustine was a very hot-blooded young man, and full of pride. Although he became increasingly aware that he was a slave to his passions, he lacked the humility to admit it and the willpower to make a change. He was like the prince in that television commercial who couldn't say no to the second potato chip, even though it meant not winning the hand of the princess. Then he discovered a whole dungeonful of suitors who couldn't say no. We can get hung up on many things that way—sex, food, an uncontrollable temper, a malicious tongue, vanity, envy, another drink. A man bumped into an acquaintance at a bar and said to him, "I thought you had given up drinking. What's the matter, no self-control?" "Sure, I've got plenty of self-control," came the reply. "I'm just too strong to be a slave to it." So we say, so we say.

Augustine was a slave to his sensual desires. They had him all boxed in and he couldn't break out. Then came the miracle of grace in that Milanese garden. St. Paul's words in Romans became the liberating word of God to him. Put on the Lord Jesus Christ, clothe yourself in his armor, defend yourself with his weapons, and break out of the box. And he was set free. God gave him the push to break loose from his bondage. It wasn't that his senses were stilled. He still had hot dreams at night and raging temptations until old age cooled him down. His writings showed this sharp sensual sensitivity for the rest of his life. But the vision in the garden, the assurance of God's nearness and help, enabled him to discipline his desires and use them to serve his higher commitments. This was a conversion of the will—not so much a surrender of resignation as a new single-minded devotion. His life and letters would now be addressed to God. "Our hearts are restless until they find their rest in thee."

Some of the changes most needed in our society are hindered by the lack of change within us. We are slaves to our appetites, our standards of living, our economic security, and therefore we limit our loving of God and neighbor for fear of losing what we have. Some young people in our time have taken the route of a greater asceticism as did Augustine, of a simpler life with less support of the military-industrial complex, less dependence upon the technological spoilers of the land, air, and water, less uptightness about open housing and helping the ghetto dwellers move out. I am not suggesting that asceticism is the way for us. To run from the city to live in the woods may be no more than a cop-out. But I do know that as long as we are slaves to our desires, giving primary attention to our sinful nature, we will never find the freedom to be really responsible for ourselves and our society, really willing to make sacrifices for our country, for others, and for ourselves.

We need a conversion of the will such as Jesus had—

"not my will, but thine, be done"; such as Augustine had—"no orgies or drunkenness, no immorality or indecency, no fighting or jealousy. But take up the weapons of the Lord Jesus Christ."

> Higher than the highest heavens,
> Deeper than the deepest sea,
> Lord, Thy love at last hath conquered;
> Grant me now my supplication,
> "None of self, and all of Thee!"

Conversion of the Intellect

There was also an intellectual conversion for St. Augustine, but it didn't happen at the same time as the conversion of his will. Augustine lived in a very pluralistic age, when the man on the street was badgered by many different reality systems. As in our own day, there were conflicting claims to truth on every hand. Today Marxism and capitalism, Zen Buddhism and "guru" cults, the Jesus freaks and Roman Catholic Pentacostals all confront us with their claims. As a result we tend to back off from a clear commitment. Who can be dogmatic about anything in these pluralistic, relativistic times? How can we say we are right and judge anybody to be wrong? So many of us flip-flop around in a state of suspended commitment, not sure of anything.

In St. Augustine's day there were "gods many and lords many." At the University of Carthage, Augustine read Cicero and became fascinated by philosophy. He was next attracted by Manicheism, a religion of good and evil wills in opposition. Augustine the student and young instructor remained attached to the Manicheans for nine years. Then in a debate with the celebrated Manichee Faustus, Augustine discovered the weakness of the Manichean system. Neoplatonism was his next love, until he came under the spell of Bishop Ambrose's preaching. Having moved to Milan, Augustine went to church and found his intellect challenged from the pulpit. Ambrose's sermons answered some of Augustine's questions about the Bible.

In other words, his intellectual conversion to the teaching of Christianity took place over a long period of time. Seeds sown in the Sunday school period at his Christian mother Monica's knee took a long time to produce a blade, a leaf, and then a full-grown ear. This intellectual conversion happened long after the moral conversion of his way of life. It is one thing to live as a Christian; it is quite another matter to think as a Christian. But by the time of his ordination as an elder, five years after the conversion of his will, Augustine's understanding of the Christian faith was pretty well set.[1] From then on he became a great defender of the faith, a protagonist extraordinary for the sovereign God of grace and the sovereign grace of God.

Augustine's greatest battle for the gospel of grace was against the English lay theologian Pelagius. "The theology of Pelagius was the theology of deism: his ethics were the ethics of naturalism." [2] He reflected the Roman

[1] Albert C. Outler, *Augustine: Confessions and Enchiridion,* Library of Christian Classics, VII (Philadelphia: The Westminster Press, 1955) , p. 19.

[2] John Burnaby, *Augustine: Later Works,* Library of Christian Classics, VIII (Philadelphia: The Westminster Press, 1955) , p. 192.

legal environment within the Western church which had been fixed by the lawyer-theologian Tertullian and the ecclesiastic Cyprian a century earlier. There was no room in Pelagius' "version of Christianity for 'Christ in you, the hope of glory,' nor for the real indwelling of the Holy Spirit in the believer. Augustine saw that in such a version the Gospel has disappeared." [3]

Taking his stand on St. Paul's Romans (see his "Spirit and the Letter"), the Doctor of Grace points us unerringly toward the unmerited love and favor of God as the ground for our salvation. This grace touches our inmost heart and will, even as it found and renewed Augustine. Grace draws and raises us to repentance, faith, and praise. It transforms our balky will so that we are capable of doing good. It relieves our religious anxiety by forgiveness and the gift of hope. It establishes our humility by cutting down our pride. God's grace became incarnate in Jesus Christ, and it remains immanent in the Holy Spirit in the church. When under severe challenge, Augustine kept Christianity close to St. Paul's gospel of grace in Romans.

Until his death at the age of seventy-six, when the Vandals were besieging his episcopal city of Hippo in North Africa, Augustine continued to expound and defend the faith. His collected works today fill fifty huge volumes, some worthless, some very profound. We shall always be indebted to him for his elaboration of the great Pauline themes which he passed on to the medieval and modern worlds.

[3] *Ibid.*

Unite Knowledge and Piety

In the lobby of the chapter house of the Augustinian Order in Paris, there are two symbols combined which characterize St. Augustine—a flaming heart and an open book. Intelligence and willpower. Someone has said that it is impossible to underrate human intelligence, especially our own. Augustine was an egghead, but despite his intellectualism he was the father of Western Christian piety, "the teacher of all who are unable to live by argument alone." [4]

We need to hang these symbols on ourselves: a flaming heart and an open book; an adoring, committed love for God that puts our wills in his way; and a commitment of our minds so that we may understand and share the meaning of Christ with modern man.

---

[4] Gerald Bonner, *St. Augustine of Hippo* (Philadelphia: The Westminster Press, 1963), p. 10.

10 God's Meat-ax

The Age of Anxiety

A Los Angeles psychiatrist maintains that since 1957 American youth are no longer anxious about survival. The mentality of the depression, which worried about starvation, is a thing of the past, he says. Not many kids these days have slaved away on a rocky farm for ten years just holding their own. "I started here on nothin'," said a grim-faced Yankee farmer, "and I got nothin' now." Today, instead of survival, we are concerned about identity: Who am I? Why am I here? Where am I going? At least, so says this specialist in adolescent behavior. A Chicago theologian insists that the Age of Anxiety has become an age of apathy. We do not need justification from above so much as a moral motivation for responsibility in daily conduct.

Well, I am not so sure that there is less anxiety today than in times of depression and world war. It seems to me we are terribly uptight about all kinds of public and private problems that threaten our survival. Crime and pornography, family failure and economic bust, crisis and confrontation, intimidate us on every front page and picture tube. The popularity of *The Sensuous Man* and *What Every Woman Should Know about Men (Sexually)* seems to suggest a widespread feeling of sexual anxiety. An escalating military budget spells worry about nuclear war, or at least worry about the survival of some industries. Student crusaders, embittered blacks, frustrated feminists, and the organized poor are sufficiently anxious about their own oppression to become militant and vocal. Could it be that the pressure of accelerated change, of denser population, of war, inflation, and injustice, is knotting our nerves and biting the fingernails of our inner composure?

Martin Luther lived in another age of anxiety. The old authorities—church and empire—were giving way to a new nationalism. Feudalism was being replaced by capitalism. Columbus had discovered the New World. Copernicus insisted that the sun, not the earth, was the center of the universe. Gutenberg's printing press was getting this distressing word around in what amounted to a communications revolution. The old dependables were tottering, and people were suffering from "future shock" in western Europe. The sixteenth century was a world filled with demons and devils, saints and sinners, Jesus the judge and Mary the merciful. The woodblock prints of Luther's day depicted Jesus seated on a rainbow with a fiery sword issuing from his mouth to smite the wicked. What was it but anxiety which would lead Luther, as a university student, to cry out in terror when struck to the ground by a lightning strike, "St. Anne, help me! I will become a monk"? The spot is marked today by a monument in a meadow outside Stotternheim, East Germany.

The Search for Salvation

So, with a sense of lostness and loneliness, not know-
ing what to count on or whom to trust, afraid and full
of despair, Martin Luther entered the Augustinian monastery in Erfurt, determined to try the ways of salvation
prescribed by medieval Catholicism. To take the cowl
and live in a cloister—poverty, chastity, obedience—all
this spelled a higher way to favor with God than the
compromised, worldly way of laymen—possessions, sex,
and doing as they pleased. If there were a way to make
yourself holy and acceptable to God, this was it. Martin
would be an athlete of the spirit, a rigorist, taking
heaven by storm. There were seven hours of canonical
prayer, day and night, fasting, mortification of the flesh
with whips and self-denial. How about that for being a
holy Joe? The monastic way was full of Brownie points
and merit badges.

In 1510 Brother Martin was asked to represent his
Augustinian chapter in Rome. What an opportunity to
soak up the merit of the saints and martyrs in the
Eternal City! Rome had a piece of Moses' burning bush
and three hundred particles of the children slaughtered
in Bethlehem. Rome had a portrait of Christ on the
veil of St. Veronica. Rome had the chains of St. Paul
and a coin paid to Judas for betraying Christ. Rome
had the twenty-eight holy stairs which supposedly had
stood in front of Pilate's palace, the stairs Jesus had
climbed to his judgment. One who crawled up these
stairs on his hands and knees, saying the Lord's Prayer
on each step, could thereby release a soul from purga-

tory. Legend has it that when Luther reached the top stair he stood erect and said, "The just shall live by faith." In fact, he wasn't yet that far advanced and what he actually said was "Who knows whether it is so?" Dismayed by the depravity and superficiality of the Italian clergy, he was filled with growing doubt. As Luther himself remarked, he went to Rome with onions and returned with garlic. In spite of all his pious works as a monk, had he really done enough to balance his alienation from God? He didn't think so.

Another way to God provided by the medieval church was the way of the sacraments: seven sure means of grace from God to man through the clergy ordained by the successors of St. Peter. This proper pedigree of ordination giving validity to the sacraments is still what officially separates some churches. Well, Luther's first celebration of Mass was a disaster for him. How could he, a sinful mortal, presume to turn bread and wine into the body and blood of Christ? How could he speak to the living and eternal and true God?

The sacrament of confession and penance brought him no peace. His sensitive conscience could enumerate an unending list of sins against God. At the monastery in Wittenberg to which Luther had been transferred, his confessor became angry with him: "If you expect Christ to forgive you, come in with something to forgive— parricide, blasphemy, adultery—instead of all these peccadilloes." Forgiveness was granted for sins confessed. Band-aids were passed out for superficial sores. But where was the cure for the deeper infection—of the whole man in his alienation from God? Driven to despair, Luther uttered the final blasphemy to his friend and confessor, Staupitz, the vicar of the order: "Love God—I don't love him. I hate him." So here was a model monk with a bright mind and a sensitive conscience, unable to believe himself fit for anything except eternal damnation—driven to desperation by the demands of God, with no sense of God's forgiveness and fulfillment.

A Revolution in Romans

Then Staupitz wisely directed Luther to a study of the Bible. Brother Martin would study for the doctor's degree, undertake preaching, and fill the chair of Bible at the University of Wittenberg. Luther objected in every way possible. The work would kill him. "Quite all right," said Staupitz; "God has plenty of work for clever men to do in heaven." So at thirty Luther began his lectures on the Bible, first the book of Psalms and then St. Paul's Epistle to the Romans. Here Luther found his Damascus Road. Another lightning bolt hit him, but it was a lightning strike of the Spirit as he quietly studied Romans.

Whereas Luther had always feared the justice of God, Romans 1 and 3 helped him to see that the justice of God is also that mercy whereby God pronounces us just and treats us as though we were just even though we are guilty. Jesus Christ was just, and as we are identified with Jesus by faith, God can accept us as he accepts him. We are not saved by the moral law and our own good-conduct medals, for a sensitive conscience knows they are never enough. We are saved by the gracious love of God who accepts us even though we know we are unacceptable. Accept that. Trust in him. This is the faith that justifies, that makes us right with God. "The justified shall live by their faith"—not by pilgrimages and masses, authorities and institutions, sacraments and self-help. By our faith in Christ shall we be justified.

Luther's discovery in Romans detonated a revolution, and soon he was standing against church and empire even as St. Paul had stood against Judaism and Rome. Challenging the abuses of the medieval church, Luther was to say at Worms, "I cannot recant . . . I will not . . . recant. Here I stand. God help me." The Protestants were so named because they testified for this faith against all oppression. Indeed, Luther's discovery dismantled the medieval world far beyond what he ever dreamed, far beyond his own political and social conservatism. Justification by faith: it meant power to the peasants, power to the individual, power to every new community of faith, power to participatory democracy, power to live as a king over all, as the compassionate servant of all.

Luther was God's man of the hour to bring reformation in the medieval church. There were other reformers who failed. A contemporary of Luther, Erasmus of Rotterdam, also worked for reformation. He made available in print the New Testament in the original Greek, so that for the first time in a thousand years Christians could get back to the original sources. Like Luther he insisted that the church of their day had relapsed into the Judaistic legalism castigated by the apostle Paul.

Christianity, said Erasmus, had been made to consist, not in loving one's neighbor, but in abstaining from butter and cheese during Lent. But Erasmus' sharp satire against the pope and clergy never accomplished much. More than scholarly criticism and moral exhortation was needed.

It was the brash, boorish Luther, using the power of justification by faith, who brought about the reformation God wanted. Only the courage of faith, with its commitment to radical, risk-taking action, could bring a breakthrough in the ruling system of the time. Erasmus was a jeweler's tool. Luther was the Lord's meat-ax.

The Liberation of Divine Acceptance

In our age of anxiety, with the threatening powers of misused technology, the pressure of population explosion, the rapid pace of change, the shifting of old moral standards, and the search for some solid rock amid the shifting sands, Luther's discovery in Romans of God's acceptance of us in Christ can be liberating for you and me:

> A mighty fortress is our God,
> A bulwark never failing;
> Our helper he amid the flood
> Of mortal ills prevailing. . . .
>
> Did we in our own strength confide,
> Our striving would be losing,
> Were not the right man on our side,
> The man of God's own choosing:
> Dost ask who that may be?

Christ Jesus, it is he;
Lord Sabaoth, his name,
From age to age the same,
And he must win the battle.

Accept that God accepts you in Christ even though you know you are unacceptable. Face the world with all its modern devils filled. Challenge what needs to be challenged in your own life and world.

We will not fear, for God hath willed his truth to triumph through us.

11 A Quiet Revolutionary

Everyone Needs a Blanket

The struggle for security is symbolized for Americans by Linus and his blanket in "Peanuts." At one point in Linus' young life he exclaims, "I'll lose my mind before this day is over!"

Engrossed in a game of checkers with Charlie Brown, Lucy replies, "Try not to think about it."

But Linus paces the floor, saying, "I can't help thinking about it! I'm only human! Oh how I hate Mondays!"

"Relax," advises Lucy.

"How can I relax with my blanket in the wash? Why does she have to wash it anyway? It wasn't dirty!" Then, with a drill sergeant's persuasion that breaks up the checker game, Linus yells, "I gotta have that blanket!" Lucy tears out to the laundry room as Linus has a fit: "I can't breathe! The walls are closing in on me! I'm getting weak! Gasp—gasp. Help me somebody! Help me! ! ! ! *Aughhh!*" Blanket in hand, Lucy returns, crying, "Hold on! Here it comes! From the washer to the dryer to you!"

"Saved," says Linus. His blanket close to his cheek, he utters a deep sigh. Peace and assurance have come.

"I guess he'll be all right now," says Lucy to Charlie Brown. "In medical circles that is known as the application of a spiritual tourniquet!"

All of us need a spiritual tourniquet. Our lifeblood is running out and we want to be saved. We need that reassurance that a mother gives to her crying child in the dark of night: "Now, now, everything's going to be all right." On "Sesame Street" someone tells a funny face how unique he is, with his unusual ears and distinctive nose. "You are important," says the voice and a hand reaches out to pat him on the head. Then the puppet turns to the wee ones in the television audience to assure them that they too are unique, important— at least loved and appreciated by someone on "Sesame Street." We may not use religious language—"How can I know I am saved?"—but we are still preoccupied with the question, searching for security and assurance.

The Search for Assurance

John Wesley's life provides us with an example of the search for assurance. At four o'clock one afternoon he went to St. Paul's Cathedral for the vesper service. The choir sang psalm 130, "Out of the depths have I cried unto thee, O Lord. Lord, hear my voice." It expressed the deep anguish of this young man who lacked the assurance of God's love and acceptance in his heart. He had thoroughly given his head to God. Trying to love God with his mind had led him to an M.A. degree at Oxford and to ordination in the Church of England. While at the university, he used his hands for the Lord in relief projects for the poor, and visiting those in prison. School days over, he volunteered to serve as a missionary chaplain in the Georgia colony. On that trip to the New World he began to sense the barrenness of a second-hand religion accepted from outside tradition and authority and never genuinely felt as a personal conviction and commitment. In the German Moravians who traveled with him to Georgia he saw this vital assurance which he himself lacked.

One day on shipboard he had gone to the usual Moravian worship service at seven o'clock in the morning. While the Moravians were singing a psalm, a great wave broke over the frail wooden ship. The mainsail split with a crack like thunder. The water poured down between the decks. Planks shivered and falling gear crashed down on the hatches. The sailors cried out, and most of the passengers were terrified out of their senses. But the good Moravians, after looking up for a moment, went on with their psalm. They were not afraid to die. Wesley was scared to death.

Upon landing in Georgia, Wesley met a young Moravian minister by the name of August Gottlieb Spangenberg, who became very direct in his questions. "Do you know Jesus Christ?" he asked.

"I know he is the Savior of the World," replied Wesley, after a moment of painful hesitation.

"True," said the young minister, later to become a Moravian bishop; "but do you know that he has saved you?"

Wesley, still confused, could only say, "I hope he died to save me." Spangenberg came back with his first searching question: "Do you know yourself?"

Without conviction, Wesley quietly answered, "I do."

That had been in February of 1736. Now it was May of 1738. Back in England, having failed in his Georgia mission, Wesley searched for this more convincing proof of God's presence in his life. After the service in St. Paul's, he went that evening to a small group meeting of Church of England laymen in Aldersgate Street. At about a quarter before nine, while a layman was reading Luther's Preface to the Epistle to the Romans, John Wesley stood up to testify to the group that he felt his heart strangely warmed. He felt that he did trust in Christ and that he was actually saved from the law of sin and death. An assurance had been given him by the Holy Spirit that Christ had died for him, and he knew he was loved and accepted by God. Even as St. Paul describes it in Romans 8:16: "The Spirit itself beareth witness with our spirit, that we are the children of God." The Holy Spirit enables us to speak to God as our Father, and makes us inheritors with Christ of all the Father wants to pass on to his children. This sounds like Luther's discovery of grace when reading Romans. It sounds like the assurance which God wants every Christian to have.

At the close of a Methodist preacher's funeral service a few years ago, all his brother ministers were invited to form a circle around his casket. Holding hands they sang blind Fanny Crosby's hymn:

> Blessed assurance, Jesus is mine!
>   O what a foretaste of glory divine!
> Heir of salvation, purchase of God,
>   Born of his spirit, washed in his blood.

This is a blessed assurance, to know that Jesus is yours and mine—an assurance that will enable us to stand straight and tall in all the stormy gales that blow.

Proclaiming the Faith

After the assurance gained at Aldersgate, mediated by Luther's Preface to Romans, Wesley's faith and joy were something that had to be shared. Good news cannot be kept to oneself. But Wesley's preaching of biblical themes was not such as to please the rectors of the Church of England in an age grown coldly deistic. His zeal and fire were offensive to them. They shut Wesley out of their churches. At Oxford, when he returned there to preach, he was criticized and never invited back. The Bishop of Bristol said to him, "You have no business here; you are not commissioned to preach in this diocese. Therefore I advise you to go hence." But Wesley's answer to the lord bishop was "The world is my parish" —words now carved on his memorial plaque in Westminster Abbey. Returning to his father's former church at Epworth, he found himself locked out by the rector. He stood on his father's tomb, which is just at the side of the church door in the churchyard. He spoke to the assembled throng on the text "The Kingdom of God is not meat and drink, but righteousness, joy and peace in the Holy Spirit." In a way this portrays his future ministry, which was largely to be outside the church, to the masses so long forgotten by the Church of England. Field preaching became a necessity, and the crowds poured forth from the mines and factories in the thousands to hear the word of God preached by John and sung in the six thousand hymns of his brother Charles. The revival spread, despite persecution and much opposition.

Conserving the Gains

Many people who had never set foot in the staid and aristocratic churches of the day responded to the gospel message. Methodist societies began to spring up in London, Bristol, and other towns and villages. Wesley defined such a society as "a company of men having the form and seeking the power of godliness, united in order to pray together, to receive the word of exhortation, and to watch over one another in love, that they may help each other to work out their salvation." Wesley himself had known the form of godliness before Aldersgate. After that experience of a warmed heart he knew the power of godliness as well. This twofold emphasis he kept central in the Methodist societies. There was only one condition required of anyone for membership: that they have "a desire to flee from the wrath to come, and to be saved from their sins." Those who desired to continue as Methodists were expected to evidence their desire for salvation: first, by doing no harm to God and man; second, by doing good of every possible sort and as far as possible to all men; third, by attending upon all the ordinances of God—that is prayer, bible reading, worship and the sacraments. These rules remain with us today and signify the high moral standards set by the early Methodists. The Methodist movement was more than just a wave of religious enthusiasm. It demanded a pure motive, a joyful experience, and a blameless life.

A Spreading Fire

The preaching and singing of repentance, justification by faith, new life in Christ Jesus, and witness of the spirit gradually swept over England, Scotland, Wales, Ireland, and on to America—meeting first with severe opposition, and later with gracious acceptance. At the time of Wesley's death in 1791 there were 313 preachers, 119 circuits and mission stations, and 76,968 members of the Methodist societies in Great Britain. In the United States 97 circuits, 698 preachers, and 46,265 members were included in the fledgling new church called Methodist. The evangelical revival had permeated the lower strata of society and effected a moral revolution.

In 1913 Élie Halévy wrote an essay crediting John Wesley with the prevention of violent revolution in England. Certainly eighteenth-century Britain was as ripe for revolt as the American colonies and Bourbon France. The common man was alienated by the tyranny of the nobility. The Enlightenment doctrines of liberty, equality, and fraternity fed the dissent. The workers in the new industries of the so-called Industrial Revolution were treated with contempt by both church and state. Working among these lower classes, Methodists were feared as potential rebels by the Establishment. Unsuccessful attempts were made in Parliament in 1811 to restrict Methodist lay preachers for fear of their possible political activism. Actually the Methodists following Wesley were quite conservative in their politics. And the empowerment of the masses to be new creatures in Christ, and the moral renewal which followed, defused any possibility of violent revolution. A quiet revolution resulted. The energies of the working man were redirected into channels of religious and social reform. A new consciousness developed which gave rise to most of the social and philanthropic thrusts of the early nineteenth century in the English-speaking world.[1] Freed by the gospel of grace, Wesley and his successors were able to turn to the needs of their neighbor. The abolition of slavery, prison reform, temperance societies, the founding of hospitals, schools, and orphanages—all of these flowed from Wesley's warmed heart. The "knight of the burning heart" launched his own special revolution: "to reform the continent and spread scriptural holiness throughout the length and breadth of the land." Assurance in the heart leads to helping hands and busy feet. Motivation then ministry is the way to lasting personal and social change.

"You seem a very temperate people here," said a nineteenth-century visitor to Cornwall. "How did it happen?" As if looking into the distant past, the old Cornishman bared his head and said quietly, "There came a man amongst us, and his name was John Wesley."[2] He was the quiet revolutionary.

---

[1] Élie Halévy, *The Birth of Methodism in England* (Chicago: University of Chicago Press, 1971), pp. 18 ff.

[2] Leslie F. Church, *Knight of the Burning Heart* (Nashville & New York: Abingdon-Cokesbury Press, 1953), p. 152.

12 Ringing the Bells of
All Christendom

On a quiet uphill street near a very contemporary
Roman Catholic church in Basel, Switzerland, proud
citizens point out the modest home of the greatest theologian of this century, and perhaps the greatest Protestant theologian since Martin Luther and John Calvin
in the sixteenth century. That house holds a second-
floor study in which were written many of his 406
published works. These include the thirteen volumes of
Church Dogmatics, containing over six million words
on seven thousand pages. On the walls of that study
hang, at the same level, two portraits, of Calvin and
Mozart. But above these at a higher level hangs Matthias
Grünewald's famous painting of John the Baptist pointing to the crucified Christ. Like John the Baptist, Karl
Barth always tried to be a witness.

In 1911, at the age of twenty-five, Barth returned from
his theological studies in Germany to enter the pastoral
ministry of the Swiss Reformed Church. The theological
climate of his training had been the skeptical liberalism
characteristic of the day, with more of an emphasis upon
the religion of man than on the revelation of God. Take
the Grünewald painting. Suppose we were to ignore the

Man on the cross and focus primarily on John the Baptist, John the beloved disciple, and the two Marys. Suppose we were to reduce faith to their religious experience. Instead of looking at Christ we look at them; thoroughly examine their feelings, their thoughts, their experiences. We soon become fascinated with our own religiosity.

Back to the Bible and Forward

This was the problem facing young Pastor Barth as he approached the pulpit of his parish church in Safenwil, Switzerland. His training had led him to believe that he could preach only what he had personally experienced. At twenty-five years of age he had very little to say. Therefore, he began to study the Bible, especially St. Paul's Epistle to the Romans. Like John the Baptist in Grünewald's painting, the Bible pointed him toward Jesus Christ, the victor on the cross. Soon he discovered that the Bible is not about a person's experience of religion, our searching for God. The Bible is about God's revelation to humanity, God searching us out in Jesus Christ.

In 1919 Barth, still a pastor in this small parish of Safenwil, published a commentary on the Epistle to the Romans, which followed St. Paul in pointing men away from all their religious idolatries and toward God in Jesus Christ. The commentary caused a furor and started a major shift in Protestant theology, and the church's radical reappraisal of its own life and mission. As

Barth later reflected upon his course, he described himself as one who was ascending a dark church tower. Trying to steady himself he reached for the bannister. He got hold of the bell rope instead. And suddenly he had to listen to the great bells sounding over him, and over all of Europe as well. Barth rang the bells of all Christendom with his rediscovery of the gospel of Jesus Christ in St. Paul's Epistle to the Romans. He turned men and women around from looking primarily at themselves to a focus on the word of God in preaching, in the Bible, and preeminently in Jesus Christ.

Church-State Struggle: The Threat of Tribal Religion

The Epistle to the Romans in 1919 and its second edition in 1922 led Barth to forty years of theological teaching and writing, first in Germany and later in his native Switzerland. These were the years of Hitler's rise to power in Germany. In those days, it was said, five Germans sat at a coffee shop table, each thinking his own thoughts. One of them sighed; another groaned aloud. The third man shook his head despairingly, and the fourth man choked down his tears. The fifth man, in a frightened voice, whispered, "My friends, be careful! You know it is not safe to talk politics in public." In such a climate of fear and intimidation Hitler swept many gullible Protestant and Roman Catholic churchmen with him. For if your basis of decision, your standard of reference, is no more than your own shared religious experiences, where can you stand? If you are always trying to accommodate the gospel to what is modern and contemporary, then anything in politics and social life can be justified. As Hitler took over Germany he made clear that there would be freedom for all religious denominations in the state "so far as they are not a danger to it and do not militate against the morality and moral sense of the German people." German Christianity was to be Aryan, anti-Semitic, and nationalistic. The Vatican made its peace with the Nazis in 1933, and in October of that year, when celebrating the 450th anniversary of Luther's birth, the German Protestant bishops capitulated. "We German Protestant Christians," they said, "accept the saving of our nation by our leader Adolf Hitler as a gift from God's hand." Karl Barth protested, but most of the German church bureaucracy supported Hitler, including his attempts to purge our Christian heritage of Jewish elements.

In response to the takeover of the German state church by Nazism, Barth and his friends came out with a new theological journal violently protesting the sellout of the German Christians and the official church. Seventeen thousand copies of the journal were sold in a single month, rallying pastors and church boards around the sovereignty of God and the lordship of Jesus Christ over church and state. In May of 1934, at Barmen, a new church was organized around a six-point confession of faith diametrically opposed to identifying the Christian message with national-racial politics. The statement was drawn up by Karl Barth and Hans Asmussen. Though the Barmen Confession did not represent even a majority of the Christians in Germany, it did serve as the rallying point for the heroic resistance of the Confessing Church. Hundreds of men, like Martin Niemöller, a former World War I U-boat captain, went to prison. Others, like Dietrich Bonhoeffer, died in concentration camps along with six million Jews.

The Confessing Church knew that it was dealing with a demonic principality and that Adolf Hitler was an anti-Christ. The theology of the Epistle to the Romans and Barth's commentary enabled men like Niemöller to oppose Hitler, saying, "Only God is my Fuehrer." So your theology, your faith-seeking-understanding, can make a tremendous difference in your own life, in the church, and in society.

It didn't take long for Hitler to catch on where his chief opposition lay. It wasn't in the universities or the press. It was among these Confessing churchmen whose intellectual leader was a Swiss democrat. Karl Barth was kicked out of the country. But he didn't go far. He accepted the chair of theology at the University of Basel, just over the border from Germany. From there he wrote letters to the churches all over Europe, spelling out the idolatry of Hitlerism and urging the Czechs, the French, the Dutch, the Norwegians, the English, and even the Americans, to resist. These letters, circulated secretly, were considered the worst kind of anti-Nazi literature.

Leave Them to Heaven

On the defeat of the German Reich, Barth encouraged compassion rather than vindictiveness, reconstruction rather than retaliation, toward the Germans. These were the words of a biblical prophet, of a St. Paul in Romans 12, who knows that God's judgment and wrath against sinful men and nations are tempered with mercy for the repentant. The Confessing Church in Germany was repentant. In 1945, at the time when Nazi war criminals were denying their guilt at Nuremberg, the leaders of the Confessing Church issued a public confession of sin. To members of the World Council of Churches meeting with them at Stuttgart, Niemöller and others confessed their involvement with their nation in a "great community of suffering but also in a solidarity of guilt." Such an attitude indicated divine healing, and opened the doors for the reconstruction of the German church and people.

Are there lessons we can learn from the state-church struggle in Germany? Some American Christians feel that these lessons apply to the struggle of churchmen with our own government over the Vietnam war and American imperialism in Southeast Asia, and South America for that matter. And what shall we say about the government's attempt to silence all criticism of its deceptive foreign policy? Are the Berrigan brothers the Niemöllers and Barths of the American church-state struggle? The Epistle to the Romans, with its message of freedom from the tyranny of all earthly powers, its message of God's sovereignty alone, the sovereignty of his judgment and grace in Jesus Christ, has inevitable social and political consequences. But if you point to the state-executed Christ as God's victor over all, then you must be willing to accept risky, revolutionary consequences with him. Jesus was executed by the political and religious powers of state and church.

Barth on the Cold War

Thus far we can salute Karl Barth for his return to the message of God's revelation and his consequent stand against the Nazi idolatry. His position seems compatible with our theological and political stand. Therefore, he is A-OK. But suppose he takes a position which is opposed to our politics. After World War II Barth became increasingly concerned about reconciliation between the hostile camps of East and West. And more often than not he was more critical of the West than he was of the East. He saw more danger in a hostile anti-Communism than in Communism itself. He was especially disturbed when the Christian West tried to make the Cold War into a holy war and branded "collective man" of the East as a demon of darkness and the "organization man" of the West as an angel of light. In the days of John Foster Dulles and Konrad Adenauer he pleaded for the churches to be bridges of reconciliation over the troubled waters dividing East and West. He saw the Christian witness of the churches behind the Iron Curtain to be a vital one without their having to become spokesmen for the politics of the West. Strange, isn't it, that President Nixon, who began his political career in those days as a fighter against Communist infiltration into American life, now builds bridges to Red China and the Soviet Union? This is what Karl Barth was trying to do twenty years ago in the midst of our anti-Communist hatred and hysteria. Perhaps if we had taken his advice then toward a greater brotherhood, a wiser reconciliation and accommodation, the Vietnam war would never have happened and the arms race would have tapered off.

Here is another instance in the life of Barth where his obedience to the word of God gave him a place to stand above the shifting sands of political, cultural, and racial change. This is not to say that the Bible gives us the latest decisions for politics. But it does give us a place to stand in the sovereignty of God, freed from the tyranny of a thousand claims to our allegiance. "Do this, do that. Be this, be that," we are told repeatedly by church and state, by television and radio, movies and books, by public opinion and presidential pleading. *No!* That way leads only to confusion and chaos. Rather, "be still and know that I am God." "I am the Lord your God. You shall have no other gods before me. . . . You shall not make yourself a graven image," whether it be the Nazi flag or the American flag, the color of your skin or the pressure of your contemporaries to swill and swagger like a pig. "You shall not bow down to them or serve them."

On December 9, 1968, at the age of eighty-two, Karl Barth died. Along with Augustine, Luther, and Wesley, he was another great revolutionary raised by Romans for obedience to the word of God in our time. Like John the Baptist, Karl Barth pointed to Jesus Christ throughout his life. His massive *Church Dogmatics* will point the way to Christ for centuries ahead. He calls us to be witnesses, not for ourselves, but for Christ; not for our nation, but for Christ; not for our race, but for Christ; not for the latest ideology of Left or Right, but for Christ, convinced that all these other things will fall into place behind this supreme loyalty.

We can conclude his life and begin our own with the closing words of St. Paul's epistle: "Let us give glory to God! He is able to make you stand firm in your faith, according to the Good News I preach, the message about Jesus Christ" (TEV). Stand firm in your faith. Preach the Good News. Give glory to God.

Postlude

The opening work commissioned for the John F. Kennedy Center for the Performing Arts in Washington, D.C., was Leonard Bernstein's *Mass*. Bernstein sees his theater piece for singers, players, and dancers as a reaffirmation of faith in the gospel of Christ. One of the most moving parts of the *Mass* is the Epistle-readings showing the trials and tribulations of Christians in the first and twentieth centuries.

The celebrant addresses the congregation from across the altar symbolic of Christ's suffering love. He tells them of the gospel he preaches and the imprisonment he has suffered in its service. But though the messenger may be jailed, God's word cannot be imprisoned.

Next we hear two readings by young men. One reads a letter from the New Testament from I John 3:13–14 (NEB): "My brothers, do not be surprised if the world hates you. We for our part have crossed over from death to life; this we know, because we love our brothers. The man who does not love is still in the realm of death, for everyone who hates his brother is a murderer."

The second youth reads a letter he has written to his parents affirming the decision he has made. We are not told what it is.

Then celebrant and chorus begin to sing a song celebrating the unfettered Word. "You can lock up the bold men" and stifle adventure and smother hope, but you cannot jail the Word of the Lord. The Word of the Lord was the creative force at the beginning of heaven and earth, and in spite of all opposition this creative Word is slowly winning its way in history.

Again there is a reading from a New Testament letter, I Corinthians 3:1; 4:9–13 (NEB), by an older man: "My brothers . . . it seems to me God has made us apostles the most abject of mankind. . . . We are roughly handled; we wander from place to place. . . . They curse us, and we bless; they persecute us, and we submit to it. . . . We are treated as the scum of the earth, the dregs of humanity, to this very day."

Then a young girl reads a letter to her parents. Today she has seen her Jim at the prison. Through the bars they talked of their marriage, and their separation because of his conscience. He is allowed no books except his Bible and prayer book. With the background of the Vietnam war, one supposes he is imprisoned because he will not cooperate with the government conscription for the killing in Southeast Asia.

Again the celebrant and chorus sing of the contradictions in a society of science and law which tries to, but cannot, abolish God's Word. For whatever be the powers entrenched, the thousands of regimes dedicated to folly and futility, the Word of the Lord persists. And mankind waits for the season, the *kairos,* the fulfillment of the Word of the Lord.

The music of the Epistle ends in an unresolved chord, a statement of impending development, anticipated action, a revolution yet to come.